This book will put fire in your heart or a pebble in your shoe; but then Jesus always does. Written by a historian, for sceptics or believers, these letters are accessible, honest, powerful and life changing. In them you'll meet the Jesus of historical fact, and the author's obsession may become your own. I just wish Christopher Hitchens could have read it.

John Ellis
Consultant Opthamologist, Dundee, Scotland

David Robertson is so honest, acute and convincing, that I fear books like *Magnificent Obsession* will soon be banned by the new atheist censors, lest enquiring young sceptics presume to examine them.

Dick Lucas
Formerly Rector, St Helen's Bishopsgate, London

David Robertson's letters are engaging and insightful. In these chapters a portrait of Jesus emerges that is attractive and compelling. This book is useful no matter what your experience and where you stand on matters of faith.

Tim Keller
Founding Pastor, Redeemer Presbyterian Church,
New York City, New York

David Robertson is a thoughtful and provocative debating partner. In a society where cultural relativism prevails, David is an unashamed Christian evangelist. David and I disagree on a great many things, but we are unified in understanding the importance of this ongoing debate.

Gary McLelland
Atheist, blogger and secular campaigner, Edinburgh, Scotland

David Robertson has done it again. Building on his incisive response to Richard Dawkins' atheism in *The Dawkins Letters* David has written another series of letters explaining how to respond to friends who say there is no proof for God. In his usual vigorous and engagingly personal manner David explains precisely why the Christian teaching about Jesus is intellectually, morally and emotionally credible. This is a book for you to read and give away. I therefore recommend that you buy as many copies as you can.

John Lennox
Professor of Mathematics, University of Oxford,
Fellow in Mathematics and Philosophy of Science,
Green Templeton College, Oxford

My dad wrote a book. It's pretty great.

Becky Milburn
New South Wales, Australia

I love this book! It's an excellent, conversational introduction to Christianity for non-Christians and new Christians who are wrestling with questions about Jesus, the Bible and the Christian church. Robertson brilliantly interacts with atheist objections and explains why Jesus is the magnificent obsession for hundreds of millions.

Jon Bloom
President, Desiring God, Minneapolis, Minnesota

David Robertson's *Magnificent Obsession* is a Christ-exalting and Christ-centred apologetic. Beautifully written, laced with tasteful humour, here is a book you can give to your non-Christian friends.

R. T. Kendall
Minister, Westminster Chapel (1977-2002), London

David Robertson's speaking ministry and books are informed, insightful, full of wit and yet surprising depth. Robertson helps us to answer the common questions of skeptics with sensitivity, astuteness and a careful listening ear.

Rebecca Manley Pippert
Prominent speaker and author,
Founder, Salt Shaker Ministries

It's outstanding. You will want to read this book and give it away to people. The subject is Jesus – a unique person in history and the ultimate defeater apologetic! You cannot argue about the character, life and message of the authentic Jesus of Nazareth.

The book has the feel of being written by a man who almost died and has discovered what or who is really important. Dragons have been slain, elephants in the room exposed and becoming a disciple of Jesus becomes totally logical and liberating.

Robertson knows Jesus and he knows our culture but just as important, he is an expert bridge-builder between the two!

David Meredith
Chairman of *Affinity* and
Minister, Smithton Free Church, Inverness, Scotland

MAGNIFICENT OBSESSION

WHY JESUS *IS* GREAT

DAVID ROBERTSON

CHRISTIAN
FOCUS

Unless otherwise stated, Scripture quotations are taken from the *Holy Bible, New International Version.* Copyright © 1973, 1978, 1984 by Biblica. Used by permission of Zondervan. All rights reserved.

Scripture quotations marked KJV are taken from the *King James Version.* All rights reserved.

David Robertson, author of *The Dawkins Letters* and *Awakening*, is pastor of St Peter's Free Church of Scotland. Robertson is a trustee of the Solas Centre for Public Christianity and works to fulfil the Centre's mission to engage culture with the message of Christ.

Copyright © David Robertson 2013

paperback ISBN 978-1-78191-271-3
epub ISBN 978-1-78191-310-9
Mobi ISBN 978-1-78191-311-6

First published in 2013
by
Christian Focus Publications Ltd,
Geanies House, Fearn, Ross-shire
IV20 1TW, Scotland
www.christianfocus.com

Cover design by DUFI-ART.com
Printed by Bell and Bain, Glasgow

CONTENTS

In Memory of

David Jack

INTRODUCTION

Now let me at the truth that will refresh my broken mind.

Mumford & Sons, *The Cave*

'I would believe if I had the evidence' is the oft-repeated and not unreasonable claim that many make when it comes to God. What is unreasonable, though, is when the statement is made with the assumption that there is either no or insufficient evidence. Bertrand Russell was once asked; 'Lord Russell, what will you say when you die and are brought face to face with your Maker?' He replied without hesitation: 'God,' I shall say, 'God, why did you make the evidence for your existence so insufficient?' This book is written to challenge that assumption.

I once had the privilege of debating with the English comedian Marcus Brigstocke on Premier Christian Radio's 'Unbelievable' show. He was perceptive, receptive, open and searching. 'Though I seek to express myself through comedy a lot of the time, there are some things I'm deadly serious about, and the desire for a workable and available deity in my life is one of them.'[1] This book is written for Marcus and those like him. I too am deadly serious about showing who God is.

In 2007 I wrote a response to Richard Dawkins's *The God Delusion* entitled *The Dawkins Letters*, little suspecting how much interest this would generate. Having spoken widely in Scotland, the U.K. and many parts of Europe and the U.S.A., I am intrigued and greatly encouraged that there is such interest in religion in general and Christianity in particular. The New Atheists thought that they were going to offer the *coup de grâce* to a religion that was dying. Instead they seem to have woken up not only the church, but many outside it, who are now beginning to think about questions they would not have contemplated a generation ago. If you are one of them, welcome to a new world. Welcome to a world of hope and the possibility that you are more

---

1. Marcus Brigstocke, *God Collar* (London: Transworld Publishers, 2011), p. 52.

than just a blob of carbon floating from one meaningless existence to another. Welcome to a world of truth, meaning and love. Welcome to a world where you will find who you really are and why you are really here. These are grand claims but I hope and pray that as you read this, your mind will be blown at the staggering wonder of the truth. I pray that you will not only gain an understanding of why so many people continue to believe in God, but also that you will come to have your own faith challenged. I realize, of course, that if you are an agnostic or atheist, you will claim that you do not have a faith, but allow me to point out that in fact all of us have a faith position – including you. There are many things you believe and act upon that you cannot absolutely prove. More of which later.

This book began life as a response to the late Christopher Hitchens's *God is Not Great,* but has morphed into something much more. It really is my answer to the question I was asked by the leader of an atheist society at a Scottish university: 'Okay, I admit you have destroyed my atheism, but what do you believe?' I was there to address a mixed group of atheists, pagans and Christians, as well as not quite sure and wannabe Christians. It was a sincere question and one that I have heard many times over the past few years. I can give many reasons as to why I am a theist (I list ten of them for example in *The Dawkins Letters*) but only one as to why I am a Christian. The clue is in the name: I am a Christian because of Jesus Christ. And therein lies the problem. What does that mean? Is it anything more than a mere Christian soundbite?

It is to answer that question that these letters have been written. They are addressed to a person whom I call 'J'. Unlike Jesus, 'J' is not real, but is rather a conflation of many of the people whom I have had coffee with, corresponded with or just generally chatted with about these things. Every question in these letters is a real one from a real person. And I suspect that many of them are questions that you have had. At the very least, I hope that you are a person who asks questions, rather than just presupposing that you know the answers. The story is told of a Christian student in the University of Edinburgh who thought he would be what Christians call 'a good witness' by going into his philosophy lecture early and writing on the blackboard 'Jesus is the Answer', before heading out of the lecture theatre. (This was some time ago – if you are under forty ask an older person what a blackboard is!) When he returned with his fellow students he was somewhat pleased to see that his chalk-written words were still there for all to see. But underneath someone had written 'What's the question?' I do believe that Jesus is the answer, in a way that goes far deeper than you can possibly hope or imagine, but we first have to ask the questions. As we look at who Jesus is, we will find ourselves being provoked to ask the questions that really matter, and hopefully will see how incredible and wonderful the answer of Christ is.

You will note that what I am *not* doing is saying, 'Just believe in Jesus'. You can't believe, you can't have faith, without knowing something about the one you are to believe in. Blind faith is a rather successful lie put about by the Father of Lies (the devil, not Dawkins!). Faith by definition is not blind. Or at least Christian faith by definition is not blind. We believe because we see Jesus. It is not so much this intangible thing called 'faith' that matters, but rather whom the object of our faith and trust is in. What I want to do is present you with the evidence for Jesus Christ in the hope that you will come to see. As John Newton, the converted former slave trader, wrote in his most famous hymn, *Amazing Grace,* 'I was blind but now I see.'

The other difficulty that so many people have is the question of truth. Indeed they often give up in despair. Like Pilate, we ask 'what is truth?' and like Pilate we too think that it is impossible to be sure of truth. So we shrug our shoulders and walk away certain only of one thing – that what we cannot know is not worth knowing. This is another lie that has caused so much of our culture to be mired in cynicism and bogged down in the quagmire of relativism. But what if there is truth and that truth is found in a person – the One who said, 'I am the Truth'? Like Albert Camus, I have a passion for an absolute and beautiful truth. I do so because, like Mumford & Sons, I believe that there is a truth that will refresh not only our broken minds but also our broken bodies, hearts and societies.

Let me add a qualification. When we say that we can know Christ we are not claiming to know *everything*. Christopher Hitchens asserts: 'And yet the believers still claim to know! Not just to know, but to know everything.'[2] Either Mr Hitchens has met some very odd Christians (not impossible I know) or he was not quite telling the truth. I have never come across any believer who believed that they *could* know everything, never mind that they did. However, we do claim that we can know, and are known by, the One who knows everything.

When we claim to know God, or that God is knowable, we are not setting ourselves up as the ultimate judge. We use 'know' in the sense of relationship with, rather than knowledge about, a subject. Herein lies the arrogance and faith of those who think they have the ability to sit in judgment upon God – our finite minds daring to think we can critique His infinite one. 'The arrogance that would make God an object and impose our laboratory conditions upon him is incapable of finding him. For it already implies that we deny God as God by placing ourselves above him, by discarding the whole dimension of love, of interior listening; by no longer acknowledging as real anything but what we can experimentally test and grasp. To think like that is to

2.   Christopher Hitchens, *God Is Not Great* (London: Atlantic Books, 2007), p. 10.

make oneself God. And to do so is to abuse not only God, but the world and oneself too.'[3]

This notion, that we have not only the ability but the right to judge the character as well as the very existence of God, is deeply ingrained in our culture. I think of the eleven-year-old boy from Huddersfield who asked: 'What do I tell my friends who say there is no proof for God?' I suspect that his friends have not engaged in deep philosophical study nor been regular attenders at church. They are just repeating the 'meme' of our atheistic culture, which both assumes that there is no proof and that we are capable of making the judgment that there is no proof.

The wonderful Roman Catholic writer G. K. Chesterton wrote: 'My own case for Christianity is rational; but it is not simple. It is an accumulation of varied facts, like the attitude of the ordinary agnostic. But the ordinary agnostic has got his facts all wrong. He is a non-believer for a multitude of reasons; but they are untrue reasons.'[4] My own case for Jesus Christ is rational. It is not simple, but an accumulation of varied facts. It is climbing Mount Improbable in order to prove to you the existence and worth of Jesus. I have often met some of the more emotive and arrogant atheists who demand, 'Show us the evidence!' The trouble is that they are not asking

---

3.   Pope Benedict XVI, *Jesus of Nazareth: From the Baptism in the Jordan to the Transfiguration* (London: Bloomsbury Publishing, 2008), p. 37.

4.   G.K. Chesterton, *Orthodoxy* (London: Hodder and Stoughton, 1999), p. 222.

a question but making an accusation. They are declaring there is no evidence and, therefore, that everything you say will automatically be dismissed. It's a bit like arguing with a conspiracy theorist – you can never win because everything you say is part of the conspiracy! There are those who read this who will automatically dismiss every piece of evidence presented here, just because it does not fit their world view and faith. Their starting point is that there can be no evidence. They trawl the Internet filtering out 'inconvenient truths' just to reaffirm themselves in their faith. However, I have hope. Firstly, you are reading this precisely because you want to find out and you are a little bit more open-minded. Secondly, if you have that kind of closed mind – watch out. Christians believe in the Holy Spirit who is able to melt the hardest heart and open the eyes of the blind! He may even use what you read in these letters to draw you to Him.

Speaking of the heart, truth is apprehended and comprehended by more than just the mind. The French philosopher and mathematician Blaise Pascal's reflections on this subject are interesting: 'We know the truth, not only through our reason, but also through our heart.'[5] It is possible to feel the truth. 'The heart has its reasons of which reason knows nothing.'[6] And that truth is felt and known through

---

5.   Blaise Pascal, *Pensées*, (London: Penguin, 2003), no. 110.

6.   Ibid, no. 423.

Jesus Christ: 'Jesus Christ is the object of all things, the centre to which all things tend. Whoever knows him knows the reason for everything.'[7] Please note that this last quote from Pascal is not saying that Christians have stumbled across the theory of everything, but that we have come across the reason for everything. So real knowledge is found when we know Christ. We know in our experience and in our spirit. We know also in our mind. Which is why Calvin says that we need to stretch our minds to Christ. In Christ are hidden all the treasures of wisdom and knowledge. What is being said here is that our search for truth is holistic, involving every aspect of our being. To know the truth you need an open mind, open ears and an open heart. It is helpful, also, to belong to an open community. I say all this because my aim is that you would be convinced of, and come to know, the truth, in your heart, mind and spirit; that you would think, feel and breathe, the Truth. It is beautiful beyond belief.

How did we get the title of this book? The BBC used to have an excellent programme series called *Everyman*. One of the documentaries, *How to get to Heaven in Montana*, was a fascinating insight into the life of a Hutterite community in that wonderful State. The pastor of the group had died and his children had, in Hutterite terms, 'gone wild'. They dared to go into town, visit the cinema and even drink alcohol! Then they

---

7.   Ibid, no. 449.

had become 'born again', as a result of which a split developed in the community. The *Everyman* team spent a year with the community and recorded how the two sides lived together. It was a beautiful documentary superbly filmed, with some fascinating insights. One of these came out when the pastor's son (one of the 'Born Agains', who had become the leader of the new group) was asked by the interviewer, 'What does Jesus Christ mean to you?' I will never forget his answer. His eyes filled with tears as he quietly declared, 'Jesus? He is beautiful … He is my everything … He is my magnificent obsession.' Pascal would have agreed: 'Jesus is the centre of all, the object of all: whoever knows not him, knows nothing aright, either of the world or of himself … In him is all our happiness, our virtue, our life, our light, our hope.'[8]

But that still leaves us with the question of where we find Jesus. This was forcefully brought home to me by a reality TV episode which, unusually for such a programme, had a great deal of reality in it. It was a kind of parent swap, in which two teenagers from England – drunken, sexually promiscuous, rude and ignorant – went to live with an African-American Baptist pastor and his wife in Atlanta, U.S.A. It was a moving and fascinating programme as they struggled to understand one another and come to terms with their common humanity in a culture clash that was brutal. No more so than when

---

8.   Blaise Pascal, *Thoughts on Religion and Philosophy,* translated by Isaac Taylor (London, 1894), p. 142.

the voice behind the camera asked the young man, as he headed back to the airport, what he had made of the whole event. 'These people are all right,' he opined. 'They're really into this Jesus bloke, aren't they? Jesus – he seems all right. Where can I find Jesus in England? Is he in the yellow pages?' That question haunted and continues to haunt me. Here was a young man shown respect and love, because of Jesus, and he wanted to know where he would find Jesus in his home country. It is the key question. How can we find the real Jesus? The answer is that He has to find us. We are so ignorant of who He is that He Himself has to come and reveal Himself to us. It is as though you have arranged to meet someone at the airport but you don't know who they are or what they are like. You stand there with a piece of paper with their name on it. Then there is that wonderful moment when they approach you and identify themselves. You have been looking for them, but they are also looking to reveal themselves to you. That is what Jesus does. He is the One we are looking for; and He is the One who is looking for us. He brings enlightenment – He is after all, the light of the world.

One other thing before you read the letters. They are highly personal. Even more so because they were written after I experienced a serious illness during which I almost died. I could tell you that I walked down a dark tunnel, saw a light and met Christ, who told me to return to earth to tell people about Him. Then this book would be number one in the

New York Times best-seller list – because, yes, people are that gullible, and do prefer the sensationalism of lurid, tabloid-style super-spirituality. I could claim that, but I would be lying. Nothing so sensational happened. I was close to death, while thousands of Christians all over the world were given a strong desire to pray for me. And their prayers were answered. I was healed, thanks to the skills and care of the doctors, nurses and physios at Ninewells Hospital, Dundee, and the X-factor of prayer and the Holy Spirit. I do believe there is a purpose in my being left on this earth – both for my family, and to be able to tell people about Jesus Christ. I do not ask you to believe because of my kind of near-death experience or dream. My aim is simply to muster all the evidence I can and to point you to the beauty of the Truth, that you might come to see and experience Him for yourself. Enjoy!

> ... What in me is dark
> Illumine, what is low raise and support;
> That to the highth of this great argument
> I may assert eternal providence,
> And justify the ways of God to men.
>
> John Milton, *Paradise Lost*, I:22–26

Ask and it will be given to you; seek and you will find; knock and the door will be opened to you. For everyone who asks receives; he who seeks finds; and to him who knocks, the door will be opened. (Matt. 7:7-8)

1 / MAN

You endeavour to prove an incredible and well nigh impossible thing; that God endured to be born and become Man.

Justin Martyr, *Dialogue with Trypho*[1]

The Church has had as much difficulty in proving that Jesus was man, against those who denied it, as in proving that he was God, and both were equally evident

Pascal, *Pensées,*[2] no. 307

Dear J,

Thanks for getting in touch. It was a real privilege meeting you and hearing what you have to say. Sorry that I wound you

---

1. Alexander Roberts, et al (Eds), *The Ante-Nicene Fathers: the Writings of the Fathers Down to A.D. 325, Volume I: The Apostolic Fathers With Justin Martyr and Irenaeus* (New York: Cosimo, Inc., 2007), p. 232.

2. (London: Penguin Books, 2003).

up a wee bit, but I am thankful that you have some passion for these very important subjects. I have just read Matthew Parris, in a wonderful article in *The Spectator,* declaring that the truth is the only thing that matters. I agree. I meant what I said about Christopher Hitchens. He was a brilliant writer and makes for superb, entertaining reading. However, his book *God is Not Great* is not really his finest work. The first major mistake is in the title (an obvious cheap shot at the Islamic chant). Normally a title should tell you what a book is about. This one doesn't. Hitchens's book is all about religion, humanity's foibles and sins. There is almost nothing about God in the book at all. After reading it, I wanted to sue under the Trade Descriptions Act! Crucially, there was almost nothing in it about Jesus. Of course, Hitchens is not alone in this. Many people, including those who profess to be religious, make this major-category error. They talk about the church, culture and ceremonies but rarely mention God. So people have responded to Hitchens's book by talking about the wonders of Christianity, or Islam or whatever particular version of religion they espouse. For example, Dinesh D'Souza's book, *What's so Great about Christianity* is a magnificent exposé of the weakness of Hitchens's arguments and demonstrates clearly the benefits that the U.S.A. in particular, and the West in general, has had from the Christian faith. But it still leaves one with the impression that we are talking about a philosophy, a way of life, a religion. As I pointed out to you, this misses the point. You asked me why I believed. I gave you lots of answers (the Creation, the Bible, the church, etc.) but all of them only lead to the one ultimate answer. I believe *in* and *because of* Jesus Christ.

However, to you that just begs the question. Doesn't everyone just invent their 'own personal Jesus' (in the words of the Depeche Mode song covered by many from Johnny Cash to Marilyn Manson)? Who is Jesus? To some, He is a religious icon; to others, the first communist; to yet others, the *Godspell* image conjures up visions of a 1960s hippy chanting 'peace and love'. In our postmodern, touchy-feely world, Jesus is whoever we want Him to be. There is no objective reality at all. Hitchens, of course, recognizes this: 'Thus the mildest criticism of religion is also the most radical and the most devastating one. Religion is man-made.'[3] Indeed. Religion *is* largely man-made – humankind's vain attempt to buy a Stairway to Heaven (with apologies to Led Zeppelin). In that sense, it matters not whether the religion involves god or gods, or is just the materialistic-humanist philosophy of Hitchens, et al – it is in effect Godless. But what if there is something different? What if there is a religion that was not based on human rules and philosophy; one which is centred on a person – for real. Unless you are going

---

3.   Christopher Hitchens, *God Is Not Great* (London: Atlantic Books, 2007), p. 10.

to make the claim that you know everything, you do at least have to consider the possibility and look at the evidence. That is why I am writing you. Jesus is real.

There is (note the use of the present tense) a personal, historical, living Jesus. Most people have some awareness of the name: perhaps an idea associated with religion, some vague memory of a long-haired hippy icon, or a barefooted, white, saintly figure in a children's Bible. But the notion of Jesus being a real person, having lived in time and space and being alive today, is quite frankly one that is to many, including some professing Christians, way out of their reality zone. Sometimes I have suggested that I know that Jesus is alive and real as much as I know that my wife is alive and real – remember how shocked you were when I first said that to you? You were ready to send for the men with the white coats! I accept that this claim is usually greeted with incredulity because, quite clearly, my physical senses prove my wife (or do they? ... but we will not divert down that particular *Matrix*-like rabbit warren just now) in a way that they do not demonstrate physically the person of Jesus Christ. So in what sense can I possibly state with such confidence that I know Him and that it is possible to have a relationship with Him? Let me begin by simply asking the question: what if, instead of our reaching out to Him, Jesus reached out to us? I am not talking about you having a personal visitation in the middle of the night (how would you know that was real?). I am talking about whether Jesus really did come to this earth, and what that means.

Please allow me to cite a past Pope again: 'For it is of the very essence of biblical faith to be about real historical events. It does not tell stories symbolizing suprahistorical truths, but is based on history, history that took place here on this earth'[4]. That is why I have invited you to the *Life of Jesus* course. The author John Dickson and his friends do a superb job of setting Jesus in the historical context of first-century Israel. The reason this works, even for those who say they are not interested in history, is that it helps dispel the notion of Jesus as being some kind of mythical made-up figure. And it is very personal.

It is precisely because there is a personal, real Jesus, that we are able to have a personal, real relationship with Him. You don't begin with an imaginary relationship. You begin with the facts and the reality of Jesus. But you don't stop there. You then go on to how He relates to you and you relate to Him. The fisherman John said about his recording of the miracles of Jesus: 'These are written that you may believe that Jesus is the Christ, the Son of God, and that by believing you may have life in his name' (John 20:31). That is why I am writing—so that you may believe that Jesus *is*, and that by believing you may have life in His name.

---

4. Pope Benedict XVI, *Jesus of Nazareth: From the Baptism in the Jordan to the Transfiguration* (London: Bloomsbury Publishing, 2008), p. xv.

Let's begin at the beginning (although as we will see, the birth of Jesus was not the beginning of Jesus). When did Jesus exist? Did He really exist? Hitchens assures us that 'there was little or no evidence for the life of Jesus'[5] This is typical of the kind of rhetoric of the New Atheists. Anyone who was seriously trained in history would recognize it for what it is: ahistorical waffle, seeking to set up a meme, which at first the faithful buy into, and then transmit over the Internet as truth. Bart Ehrman, no friend of biblical Christianity, has challenged this new approach. Have a look at his YouTube trailer[6] for his book, *Did Jesus Exist?* He declares that Jesus 'was a real person and we can know some things about him' and that the evidence for Jesus is 'overwhelming'. Dickson makes the point clearly: 'Profs Gerd Theissen and Annette Merz of the University of Heidelberg in Germany – leading critical scholars and by no means advocates of Christian apologetic – write, "the mentions of Jesus in ancient histories allay doubt about their historicity".'[7] Suffice it to say for now, that the only reason that people will not accept the overwhelming evidence for the existence of Jesus is that they just really do not want Him to exist.

After speaking about Jesus in the now sadly defunct Borders store in Cambridge, I was challenged by an

5.   Christopher Hitchens, *God Is Not Great*, p. 127.

6.   http://www.youtube.com/watch?v=SB6EZzJ7m1c.

7.   John Dickson, *The Life of Jesus: Who He is and Why He Matters* (Grand Rapids, Michigan: Zondervan, 2010), p. 39.

articulate and intelligent man, in some detail, on the writings of Tacitus and Josephus as evidence for Jesus. He certainly knew what he was talking about and his comments were astute, knowledgeable and politely put. Indeed I learnt something from him, not least about the dispute on one of the quotes. I asked him about how he knew so much, and he replied: 'I am professor of biblical archaeology at the University of Jerusalem'! He was not a Christian but he said something particularly wise after that. 'I would not expect to find lots of writings about Jesus in the first century. Why? Because he was a Palestinian peasant who was executed on a cross.' His point was valid. It is the rulers and the victors who generally write history. Why would they include Jesus in that? Absence of evidence is not evidence of absence. The trouble is that our fundamentalist atheists so often fail to understand context, and as a result, it is almost as if they are demanding newsreels, DVDs, newspaper articles and e-mails from the first century to prove Christ. One man has just tweeted me demanding written news reports from A.D. 33-35 to prove Jesus existed! He clearly does not understand how history works. By any accepted historical standards, there is little doubt that Jesus existed.

At that same meeting in Cambridge, I was informed by a Swedish teacher that he agreed that Jesus existed but that He had come from another planet and that English Lords were descended from Him – hence the reason they were called Lord! I sincerely hope he was not a lecturer at the University! If the denial of the historicity of Jesus Christ borders on the fantastical, the belief that Erik Von Däneken espoused of Jesus being an alien has long crossed the border of rationality and evidence, and I will not insult your intelligence in discussing that, any more than I would spend time trying to explain to you why Jesus was not a boiled egg.

Sources

Where do we get our sources of information about Jesus Christ?

There are extrabiblical sources. Mara Bar-Serapion (A.D. 75), the Roman historian Tacitus (A.D. 115), and the Jewish historian Josephus (A.D. 90) all mention Jesus Christ. Let me give you the two most famous quotes. They are a bit lengthy but they are extraordinary. Firstly Josephus:

> Now there was about this time Jesus, a wise man, if it be lawful to call him a man, for he was a doer of surprising works, a teacher of such men as receive the truth with pleasure. He drew over to him both many of the Jews, and many of the Greeks. He was the Messiah. And when Pilate, at the suggestion of the principal men among us, had condemned him to the cross, those that loved him at first did not forsake him; for he appeared to them alive again the third day, as the divine prophets had foretold these and ten thousand other wonderful things concerning

him. And the tribe of Christians, so named for him are not extinct to this day.

This was written around A.D. 95. Some dispute parts of this quote but the basic message is the same. Secondly, Tacitus writing in A.D. 115:

The founder of this sect, Christus, was given the death penalty in the reign of Tiberius by the procurator Pontius Pilate; suppressed for the moment, the detestable superstition broke out again, not only in Judea where the evil originated, but also in the city of Rome to which everything horrible and shameful flows and where it grows.

And then there is the Bible, in particular the four Gospels. I love what Erasmus, the sixteenth-century scholar and Reformer, wrote: 'The Bible will give Christ to you, in an intimacy so close that he would be less visible to you if he stood before your eyes'[8]. This is an extraordinary claim, but in my experience I can testify to its truth. It means that there is a whole lot more to the Bible than just being history, but it is history. So let's examine what that means.

Some of your friends have told you that you cannot accept the Gospels as historical documents. Why not? They were written as historical documents (take for example the prologue to Luke's Gospel, which talks about investigating and sources).

---

8.   Erasmus, cited in John Stott, *The Incomparable Christ* (Leicester: InterVarsity Press, 2001), p. 15.

You could argue that they are bad or inaccurate history, but you cannot automatically dismiss them as unhistorical mythological, fictional documents, just because the church uses them. In order to prove that they were inaccurate, false or just mythology, you have to get through a number of hoops first. You could, for example, identify events, places or people that they describe which we now know from history did not exist. You could date the Gospels, which purport to be eyewitness – or based on eyewitness – accounts, as being centuries after the events the authors supposedly witnessed. Many have tried. And you could claim that there were many other 'gospels' and that the church in or around the fourth century just did a pick 'n' mix of the ones that suited them. So let's look at all three of these hoops.

First, let's take one example of how people have tried to prove the Gospels wrong – the question of Nazareth. All four Gospels point out that Jesus' hometown was a small place called Nazareth. For many years, 'scholars' and sceptics argued that this was a fiction because the Jewish historian Josephus did not mention Nazareth in his writings. Then, lo and behold, in the 1950s an ancient village on the traditional site was discovered. That particular argument has been blown to pieces. As indeed have many similar attempts to disprove the Bible.

Secondly, the question of dating. Hitchens argues that Jesus' 'illiterate living disciples left us no record'[9]. This set

---

9.   Christopher Hitchens, *God Is Not Great*, p.114.

me wondering how illiterate disciples could write. Hitchens, of course, pronounces that they didn't. This is just prejudice and chronological snobbery. How does he know that Jesus' disciples were illiterate? Matthew, a tax collector, would certainly not have been, neither would Luke the doctor. Mark and John could clearly read and write. The fact is that we have no substantive reason to doubt that the Gospels were written by those who were eyewitnesses of Jesus. As John puts it: 'That which was from the beginning, which we have heard, which we have seen with our eyes, which we have looked at and our hands have touched – this we proclaim concerning the Word of Life' (1 John 1:1).

Thirdly, the question of the other gospels. This particular myth has been perpetuated by the truly dreadful, *The Da Vinci Code*. When we set up a debate on the film and the book, we scoured high and low throughout Britain to find any academic who would be prepared to defend the claims made by Dan Brown that the church just selected the gospels in the fourth century and rejected a whole lot of equally valid 'gospels'. No one was prepared to. It is a fanciful myth and is taken seriously only by those who think that *The Sun* or *The National Enquirer* are reliable sources of news. I have spent the past year reading all these so called 'gospels' – at least those which have been translated into English. If you are serious about this question, then all I would suggest is that you read them and compare them with the four Gospels we have in the Bible. You will soon see the difference. 'Chalk and cheese' would not be an adequate phrase to describe how vastly different they are.

The virgin birth

But let's go on to look at some of the actual history. Probably the most important thing about the birth of Christ is what is known as the virgin birth. The television and radio host Larry King was once asked whom he would like to interview if he had his pick from all history. His answer? Jesus Christ. 'What is the one question you would like to ask him?' 'I would ask him if he was indeed virgin-born, because the answer to that would define history for me.'

Christopher Hitchens, of course, has no doubt. And you seemed to have been impressed by this. But, in reality, Hitchens's pronouncements are largely bluster. 'Matthew and Luke cannot concur on the virgin birth.'[10] His comments on Isaiah 7:14 are particularly interesting: 'The word translated as "virgin", namely *almah*, means only "a young woman".'[11] In one meeting in Belfast, there was almost a riot between some Young Earth creationists and the militant 'you-are-all-going-to-atheist-hell' secularists. When things calmed down, a young man dressed in his black goth outfit complete with chains and nose studs,

---

10. Christopher Hitchens, *God Is Not Great*, p. 111.

11. Ibid, p. 115.

shouted out from the back, 'There are hundreds of Greek, Egyptian and Roman myths about babies being born on the 25th of December, why should we believe yours?' I broke the cardinal rule of polite debating by mocking him – 'You, sir, are a prime example of the dangers of Wikipedia' – before going on to point out the fallacies within his statement. At the end of the evening he was standing at the back of a long queue, looking really angry. I took my time signing books but he was very patient and waited, and waited. When it was his turn, I shook his hand and apologized for putting him down. But he just laughed. 'No,' he replied, 'I thought you were going to give me some of that Christian XXXX, and I was going to walk out. But you called me on it. Cheers.' And off he went.

Sadly, Hitchens argues at that level. I am sorry to say that, but it is not unreasonable to treat as bluster the statements of a man who can declare that Augustine, the writer of at least two of the greatest books in human history, was 'an ignoramus'.[12] Unlike Hitchens, E. J. Young and R. D. Wilson did serious research on the meaning of the nine occurrences of *almah* in the Old Testament. Both conclude that the word is never employed to describe a married woman, and that the Septuagint (cited by Matthew's Gospel) was right to translate it in Greek as *parthenos* (virgin).

---

12. Ibid, p. 64.

Hitchens, though, is in good and bad company. There are many more 'sophisticated' clergymen who are stuck in a nineteenth-century paradigm of 'miracles don't happen' and so do their best to dismiss the virgin birth as untrue or unimportant. Tony Jordan, a scriptwriter for the BBC series *EastEnders*, did an excellent mini-series on the Nativity. He describes his experience in researching this: 'I sat with these men of the cloth, these were organized religion. They were all explaining to me about the Nativity and about how it never happened. And they were saying, "Well of course, Mesopotamia….mumble, mumble – there was always the legend of the virgin birth." And I'm thinking, "What? Hang on a minute! You're on the wrong side, that doesn't work." So I despair of them.'[13] Indeed. The 'evangelical' liberal, Rob Bell, likened the virgin birth to one brick in a wall of theology. 'What do you lose if you lose that one brick?' – to which the best reply was that of Mark Driscoll: 'Nothing, except Jesus.' The virgin birth of Christ is one of the key doctrines of Christianity and without it you do not have Christ. It's a bit like the man who goes into the local fish and chip shop and announces, 'I'll have a fish supper, without the fish'! Christianity without the virgin birth of Christ is Christianity without Christ.

I have to confess that I have never understood why the virgin birth was seen as such a stumbling block. If human

---

13.   Tony Jordan, interview in *Christianity* magazine, March 2012.

beings can manufacture a situation whereby a woman can become pregnant without the necessity of sexual intercourse, why should we consider it impossible for an almighty God to do so? He does not need IVF or a turkey baster! The trouble is that people start off with the presupposition that such a God does not exist, and therefore a non-existent being cannot perform such a miracle. This is the ultimate in circular reasoning. To claim that a virgin birth cannot happen because the Being who could make such a thing happen does not exist, really says nothing, other than about the prejudices of the person making the claim. Likewise, I am NOT stating that merely claiming it did happen makes it true. However, I AM stating that by definition it is not self-evidently impossible that an almighty God could do this miracle!

It does all make sense. So much so that there is an increasing trend amongst those who once thought sceptical atheism was the only way to fly, to turn or return to the fold. You are too young to remember this, but A. N. Wilson was one of the most famous atheists in the United Kingdom. In 1992 he wrote a popular book entitled *Jesus: A Life,* in which he argued the conformist position of the time that the Gospels were just legends. Seventeen years later, one Saturday afternoon, I was doing my usual, lying in the bath, drinking a coffee and reading *The Spectator* (in my view the magazine with the best writing of English in the world), when I had one of those 'Eureka' moments. I almost shouted for joy to read an article by the aforementioned Mr Wilson, renouncing his atheism and announcing his return to Christianity.

Tim Keller tells the story of the novelist Anne Rice, who had lost her childhood faith. When, however, she began to read the work of sceptical scholars, it had the opposite effect of restoring the clarity and simple truth of the historical, biblical Jesus. 'The whole case for the non-divine Jesus who stumbled into Jerusalem and somehow got crucified by nobody and had nothing to do with the founding of Christianity and would be horrified if he knew it – that whole picture which had floated in the liberal circles I frequented as an atheist for thirty years – that case was not made.'[14]

I leave you with that thought. Please feel free to get back to me. I am sorry that I have skimmed over these deep topics in such a quick fashion, but if you want to investigate this further then I would be happy to recommend several books for you,

Yours etc.,

David

> But when the time had fully come, God sent his Son, born
> of a woman, born under law, to redeem those under law,
> that we might receive the full rights of sons. (Gal. 4:4-5)

---

14. Timothy Keller, *King's Cross: The Story of the World in the Life of Jesus* (London: Hodder & Stoughton, 2011), p. xxi.

2 / MIRACLES

It is not possible to have reasonable grounds for not believing in miracles.

Blaise Pascal[1]

I approve your desire, my friend, and praise the zeal you manifest in the discussion of opinions. For it assuredly becomes every one who is desirous of knowledge, not simply and out of hand to agree with what is said, but to make a careful examination of the points adduced.

Maximus, Bishop of Jerusalem, A.D. 185[2]

Dear J,

Thanks for getting back to me. I am delighted that you picked up on the discussion about the virgin birth. Even

---

1. Blaise Pascal, *Pensées* (London: Penguin, 2003), no. 568.

2. Alexander Roberts, et al (Eds), *The Ante-Nicene Fathers: the Writings of the Fathers Down to A.D. 325, Volume I: The Apostolic Fathers With Justin Martyr and Irenaeus* (New York: Cosimo, Inc., 2007), p. 770.

more so that you asked the question – so what? Does it really matter? You tell me that you are not against Jesus and you don't even mind people who want to believe in Him, but what relevance does it have to you? Great question. Why should the fact that Jesus was born of a virgin matter to you at all? The answer is that, if true, it is part of the evidence that there is a God, who does 'intervene' in the world and who does call us to follow Him. If Jesus is who He says He is, then that is a game-changer, not just for the world, but for your life as well. You said, 'I would believe in God if he walked into my room just now as I write.' But He did. At least He did not walk into your room but He did walk into many rooms in first-century Palestine and many did not believe even then. 'It is true that the Christian gospel is an account, not of something that happened yesterday, but of something that happened long ago; but the important thing is that it really happened. If it really happened, then it makes little difference when it happened. No matter when it happened, whether yesterday or in the first century, it remains a real gospel, a real piece of news.'[3] Today I would claim that, because of that 'incarnation', Jesus is in my room just now as I write, through His Word and Spirit, and that is something that you can know too. But that perhaps is getting ahead of ourselves. So let's continue with our inquiries. The

---

3.   J. Gresham Machen, *Christianity and Liberalism* (Grand Rapids, Michigan: Wm. B. Eerdmans, 2009), p. 103.

Bible teaches that the birth of Jesus was truly miraculous – which brings us to the subject of miracles.

What is a miracle?

When we use the term 'miracle', we need to be very careful. We need to define terms. The word can be used very lightly. It's a miracle that you got out of bed today; it's a miracle that your football team won. But that is not what we mean when we talk about a biblical miracle. For the purposes of our discussion, let us make clear what we mean. C. S. Lewis, whose book on this subject I would highly recommend, puts it succinctly: 'I use the word miracle to mean an interference with nature by a supernatural power.'[4]

Do miracles actually happen?

The knock-down argument against the possibility of miracles is considered to be that of the eighteenth-century Scottish philosopher David Hume, who in his book, *An Enquiry Concerning Human Understanding,* devotes the whole of section ten to the question of miracles. This has almost reached the level of canonical status amongst atheists and agnostics, who often cite it as the last word. To summarize: Hume argues that miracles are single events which never have enough evidence because those who provide that evidence (human beings) can never be completely reliable.

---

4.   C. S. Lewis, *Miracles* (London: Collins Fount, 1960), p. 7.

He writes, 'No testimony is sufficient to establish a miracle, unless the testimony be of such a kind, that its falsehood would be more miraculous than the fact which it endeavours to establish.'[5] Even allowing for that disputed argument, I would be prepared to state that the miracles of the New Testament actually fit those criteria and that, given the existence of an almighty God, then Pascal's comment at the beginning of this letter is apposite: 'It is not possible to have reasonable grounds for not believing in miracles.' The trouble is the presuppositions that one brings to the argument. If you presuppose that there is no supernatural being then by definition there cannot be miracles. If you on the other hand accept the possibility of an almighty God, who is both powerful and free, then miracles are not a problem. As the Westminster Confession of Faith puts it, 'God, in his ordinary providence, makes use of means, yet is free to work without, above, and against them, at his pleasure.'[6]

At this point, then, the argument could be over. The atheist who says there is no evidence for God, but cannot accept the evidence of miracles because there is no God to perform those miracles, needs a miracle to break out of this circular thinking! Religious people who just accept that

---

5.   Quoted in John Dickson, *Life of Jesus: Who He is and Why He Matters* (Grand Rapids, Michigan: Zondervan, 2010), p. 85.

6.   The Westminster Confession of Faith, V: 3.

God works miracles find themselves in the same circular argument, and never the twain shall meet. Is there a way out of this impasse? Yes. Can I suggest we follow Christopher Hitchens, whose book began this whole conversation? 'Our belief is not a belief. Our principles are not a faith. We do not rely solely upon science and reason, because these are necessary rather than sufficient factors, but we distrust anything that contradicts science or outrages reason. We may differ on many things, but what we respect is free inquiry, open-mindedness, and the pursuit of ideas for their own sake. We do not hold our convictions dogmatically'[7]. Amen. Let us have 'free inquiry', 'open-mindedness' and let us not hold our convictions dogmatically.

I am not sure where you stand on this question. Clearly you do not believe that miracles *must* happen, but do you hold to the atheist doctrine that miracles *cannot* happen? C. S. Lewis argues that, before you look at the historical evidence for miracles, it is essential groundwork to determine philosophically whether miracles are possible at all. He accuses modern historians and Bible critics of having a cultural bias which precludes them from even allowing for the possibility of miracles. G. K. Chesterton put it beautifully: 'The believers in miracles accept them (rightly or wrongly) because they have evidence for them. The disbelievers in

---

7.   Christopher Hitchens, *God Is Not Great* (London: Atlantic Books, 2007), p. 5.

miracles deny them (rightly or wrongly) because they have a doctrine against them."[8] I have come across this so many times. It is what psychologists call confirmation bias, where we tend to look for information that confirms our bias, rather than anything which would contradict it. It is for that reason that I try to read as many atheist writers as possible. It is very hard, however, to argue with someone who just knows. I am grateful that you are a little bit more open-minded, as evidenced by your willingness to read this!

So step one is accepting that miracles are philosophically possible. As Sherlock Holmes advised Dr Watson, 'When you have eliminated the impossible, whatever remains, however improbable, must be the truth'! The question then becomes one of evidence. Actually, it becomes one of how we can ascertain and evaluate evidence. The truth is that everything we think is a matter of both reason and faith. There are some atheists who want to argue that everything they believe is determined by reason and that they have the ability to ascertain whether any evidence is admissible. But even reason is a matter of faith. As the biologist J. B. S. Haldane pointed out, the belief that our reason is just a by-product of matter is itself a statement of faith that cannot be proven:

> It seems to me immensely unlikely that mind is a mere by-product of matter. For if my mental processes are

---

8.   G. K. Chesterton, *Orthodoxy* (London: Hodder and Stoughton. 1999), p. 224.

determined wholly by the motions of atoms in my brain I have no reason to suppose that my beliefs are true. They may be sound chemically, but that does not make them sound logically. And hence I have no reason for supposing my brain to be composed of atoms. [9]

Chesterton, with greater economy of words, simply says: 'Reason is itself a matter of faith. It is an act of faith to assert that our thoughts have any relation to reality at all'.[10]

It is reasonable to accept that miracles are at least theoretically possible. But now we need more. Biblical faith is, contrary to Dawkins, et al, faith that is based upon evidence. John Humphrys buys into this atheist definition of faith. 'Which takes us back to the believer's core defence: if I could prove it, it wouldn't be faith.'[11] But that is the atheist and agnostic version of faith. The Christian version is different: 'Faith is not based on ignorance but on knowledge. Understanding is joined with faith ... unbelief in all men is always mixed with faith.'[12]

I am not asking you to have blind faith in Jesus, but rather faith based upon knowledge, incomplete though that is, and limited though our capacity to understand undoubtedly is.

---

9.   J. B. S. Haldane, *Possible Worlds and Other Essays*, 1927, (Reprint, London: Chatto and Windus, 1932), p. 209.

10.   G. K. Chesterton cited in *The Spectator,* November 2008.

11.   John Humphrys, *In God We Doubt* (London: Hodder and Stoughton, 2007), p. 190.

12.   John Calvin, *Institutes of the Christian Religion*, 3:1:2.

Did Jesus do miracles?

Here we come up with a problem of history. The trouble is that a postmodern view of history has taken a grip of many (non) thinkers. History is seen only through the eye of the recipient and, just as you can have a pick 'n' mix theology, so you can have a pick 'n' mix view of history. 'Postmodernism is a denial of the fixity of the past, of the reality of the past apart from what the historian chooses to make fit, and thus of any objective truth about the past….Postmodernist history recognizes no reality principle, only the pleasure principle – history at the pleasure of the historian.'[13] But whilst we need to be aware of our own confirmation bias, I think it is possible to read history and to find out things that did happen in the past – remembering, of course, that ultimately we cannot prove anything in an absolutist sense. However, you will find that the evidence for the miracles of Jesus is robust.

Firstly, we have the historical testimony of the Gospels themselves. As I indicated in my first letter to you, there are good reasons for taking the Gospels as historical documents. Then there is the testimony of the early church. Hume's criteria of many witnesses is met many times through this testimony, whether it was the feeding of the 5,000, the 500 who at one time saw the resurrected Christ, or the hundreds who were at the greatest funeral ever, that of Lazarus!

---

13. Historian Gertrude Himmelfarb, cited in *The Spectator*, 31 January 2009, p. 29.

The man who is known as the first of the Christian apologists, Quadratus, addressed the Emperor Hadrian in the year A.D. 124 with these astonishing words:

> Our Saviour's works, moreover, were always present: for they were real, consisting of those who had been healed of their diseases, those who had been raised from the dead; who were not only seen whilst they were being healed and raised up, but were afterwards constantly present. Nor did they remain only during the sojourn of the Saviour on earth but also a considerable time after His departure; and indeed some of them have survived even down to our own times.[14]

The early church fathers were much clearer on this than some church leaders in the twenty-first century, who, following the fashion of the age, decided that everything could and should be explained in naturalistic terms. Thus, Jesus feeding the 5,000 was really Jesus using a small boy to encourage everyone to share their hidden picnic lunches, Lazarus being raised from the dead was really him waking up from a deep coma, and Jesus walking on the water was actually Him walking on a sandbank! I honestly don't know why they bother. A Jesus who did not perform miracles, but only pretended that He did, would not be worthy of following.

---

14.   Quadratus, Bishop of Athens, in Alexander Roberts, et al (Eds), *The Ante-Nicene Fathers: the Writings of the Fathers Down to A.D. 325, Volume I: The Apostolic Fathers With Justin Martyr and Irenaeus* (New York: Cosimo, Inc., 2007), p. 749.

We have, then, a logical possibility that an almighty God could perform miracles, and historical testimony claiming that He did. I realize that that is not proof enough for most people and you can dismiss it because you do not have the video testimony (which could be faked) or are not able to time travel and see it yourself. But it is at least sufficient to dismiss the somewhat arrogant claim that 'I don't believe it, because miracles don't happen.'

The biblical case for miracles, however, goes beyond philosophy and history. It also has the ring of truth in terms of its purpose.

Why did Jesus do miracles?

> You are probably quite right in thinking you will never see a miracle done: you are probably equally right in thinking that there was a natural explanation of anything in your past life which seemed, at the first glance, to be 'rum' or 'odd'. God does not shake miracles into nature at random as if from a pepper pot. They come on great occasions; they are found at the great junctions of history – not of political or social history, but of that spiritual history which cannot be fully known by man.
>
> C. S. Lewis, *Miracles*[15]

Contrary to many people's impressions, miracles are not commonplace in the Bible. They are clustered around Moses,

---

15. C. S. Lewis, in 'Epilogue', *Miracles* (1960).

Elijah and Elisha, and Jesus. Miracles were given as signs to authenticate the messenger and usher in a new period of God's revelation of Himself.

Jesus' miracles show us His identity, His kingdom and His character. They show us His identity because, as Peter told the Jews at Pentecost, 'Jesus of Nazareth was a man accredited by God to you by miracles, wonders and signs, which God did among you through him, as you yourselves know.'[16] They reveal His kingdom, because the signs of the kingdom, which had been prophesied years before, were done through Him. When John the Baptist asked if He was the One who was to come, Jesus replied: 'Go back and report to John what you hear and see: the blind receive sight, the lame walk, those who have leprosy are cured, the deaf hear, the dead are raised, and the good news is preached to the poor.'[17] In terms of His character, they demonstrate His love – the miracles were always done for the good of people. At the feeding of the 5,000, 'Jesus called his disciples to him and said, "I have compassion for these people; they have already been with me three days and have nothing to eat. I do not want to send them away hungry, or they may collapse on the way."'[18] One of the early fake gospels, the 'gospel of Thomas', does not grasp this. It tells the story of

16. Acts 2:22.

17. Matthew 11:4-5.

18. Matthew 15:32.

a boy Jesus making clay birds and then clapping his hands and making them come to life. The Gospels tell us that even when hungry He resisted the temptation of the devil to turn stones into bread.

I think it is important to realize that most of the things Jesus did were not miracles. He did many ordinary and extraordinary things, as well as miracles. The miracle of the incarnation is seen more clearly in the fact that Jesus sawed wood, walked through villages, got dusty feet, hungered, became thirsty, had family who did not 'get' Him, was homeless, lost His dad, and wept at funerals, than it is in the miraculous signs. The miracles were a sign of who He was. They were also a message that tells us about God – not least that God is love. There are many people who over-sentimentalize the love of God. They use the words 'love of God' in much the same way that they would talk about loving chocolate. But the definition of love is God. He is love. B. B. Warfield pointed out: 'It hurt Jesus to hand over even hardened sinners to their doom. It hurt Jesus – because Jesus' prime characteristic was love, and love is the foundation of compassion.'[19] Jesus got angry at sin, injustice and death. Jesus wept. The greatest miracle of all is surely that Jesus came from the glory of heaven, emptied Himself, became a servant, became 'nothing' and lived amongst us.

---

19. B. B. Warfield, excerpt 'The Emotional Life of our Lord' from *The Person and Work of Christ,* (Philadelphia: P&R, 1950), p. 101.

I rejoice that Jesus showed His power as the Lord of creation by stilling the waves and calming the storm, I rejoice even more that He as the Creator became part of the creation, so that He could deal with the raging storm within, rescue us and restore fallen human beings to be the children of God.

The miracles and the works of Christ tell us who He is – so that we can know Him, love Him and follow Him. Which is why I am somewhat amused and bemused by the kind of comments that Hitchens makes, such as, 'Religion teaches people to be extremely self-centred and conceited.'[20] Apart from the obvious rejoinder that Mr Hitchens was not exactly known for his self-effacing humility, I think the obvious point is that people *are* self-centred and conceited, not that religion makes them such. It could be said that many religions exploit that self-centred conceit, but that cannot be said about Jesus. All His deeds demonstrate His love and call us out of our selfishness into His self-giving.

Does He still do miracles?

The question now is, were miracles only for the Gospels? I take my clue from the historian, Dr Luke, who in part two of his account of Christ (what we now know as the Acts of the Apostles) writes: 'In my former book, Theophilus, I wrote about all that Jesus began to do and to teach.'[21]

---

20. Christopher Hitchens, *God Is Not Great*, p. 74.

21. Acts 1:1.

Note the word 'began'. Jesus began His work and then, after He is taken up to heaven, He continues His work through His Spirit working in and through His church. Now we need to be careful here. Not everything that claims to be a miracle done in the name of Jesus is one. Right now you could switch on cable TV and find numerous Christian channels promising you a miracle. There is always some tele-evangelist announcing that someone has grown his or her leg, been healed of a growth, and similar. Very few announce that they have had an amputated arm replaced or a dead person raised, although there have even been exceptions to that – like the bizarre tele-evangelist Todd Bentley, who in the midst of his revival crusades, announced that several people had been raised from the dead. However, he was unable to provide verification of this because of 'patient confidentiality'! Or there was the time at a Spring Harvest conference when a woman excitedly stood up and declared to all in our group: 'They are raising the dead so much in Africa that they have had to set a limit on it!'. 'Really? You mean that when people die aged sixty they will raise them, but if they are over seventy they won't?'!

Thankfully, one of the speakers was an Anglican charismatic, who pointed out that in his travels all over the world he had often heard similar claims: when he is in Africa he hears about the dead being raised in Asia; when he is in Asia he hears about the dead being raised in America;

and when he is in America he hears about the dead being raised in Africa! Please understand that I am not arguing for that degree of gullibility. But, yes, I do believe that God still answers prayer and, yes, that sometimes these can be at the level of biblical miracles.

In the village of Brora, in the Scottish Highlands, one of the elders had a daughter who was seriously ill. Following the instruction of the Bible (in James, chapter 5) he asked his fellow elders to come and anoint her with oil and pray. After doing so, she recovered. Was that a miracle? Possibly. In the same village, the church needed £10,000 of repairs, for the repointing of all the external walls. It was £10,000 beyond their means and so they prayed. They did not receive the £10,000, but a man was converted – he turned out to be a builder – who was able, together with the other men from the congregation, to re-point the whole building for nothing. A miracle? Whilst it was certainly an answer to prayer, it was not a miracle in the biblical sense of the word.

When I came out of hospital after a critical illness from which I was not expected to recover, my surgeon told me that he regarded my recovery as 'miraculous'. There is no doubt that the skill of the surgeon, doctors, nurses and physiotherapists played a huge part in my recovery, as did the love of my family and the coincidence of my collapsing outside a doctor's surgery. But there was also another factor. Many people from all over the world were given a real desire to pray for me – for example, some people told me of being woken at three in the morning and not being able to get back to sleep until they had cried out in prayer for my healing. My whole denomination was asked one Sunday to pray for me at noon that day. From that weekend onwards, my recovery gained momentum. Coincidence? Possibly. Does it prove anything? Not necessarily. But it is a wee bit suggestive, and it was very helpful to me, not least because I am now enabled to write this to you. It was not for nothing some of the staff nicknamed me 'Lazarus'!

If you are like many people, you will sometimes be tempted to think that if only God showed you a miracle then you would believe. But is that really the case? Jesus told the story of a rich man who lived in luxury every day and ignored a beggar named Lazarus. He died and in hell he pleaded with Abraham to send Lazarus (who was standing beside Abraham in heaven) to go to warn his brothers, to which Abraham responded, 'They have Moses and the Prophets; let them listen to them.' The rich man thought that sending Lazarus would be better because he reckoned that if someone from the dead went to them they would repent – a not unreasonable assumption you would think. And yet Abraham's reply was sobering. 'If they do not listen to Moses and the Prophets, they will not be convinced even if someone rises from the dead.'[22] The bottom line is that, if

22.   Luke 16:31.

you don't believe what God says in His Word, it is unlikely you will believe even if you see a miracle. As Pascal stated, 'Miracles do not serve to convert, but to condemn.'[23]

I do believe that God can and sometimes does intervene supernaturally, often in response to the prayers of His people. But we are not to be miracle seekers, treating God as though He somehow had to prove Himself to us. He has already done so in Christ. There is one miracle, though, which I think is greater than any recorded of Jesus in the New Testament – it is a miracle I have experienced, and it is the miracle I hope and pray for you. It is called the new birth. If you read John's Gospel, chapter 3, you will read the story of a rich scholar, a theologian called Nicodemus, who came to Jesus and asked him about entering the kingdom of God. Jesus told him that he couldn't even see the kingdom of God unless he was born again of the Spirit of God. Read the chapter and you will see how amazing it is. The bottom line is that we need God to regenerate us (I know it sounds like a Dr Who plot – but it's true), to create in us a new heart, to give us new life. And this is precisely why Jesus came – to grant us that life. It is my prayer that you will receive and accept that new life,

Yours etc.,

David

---

23.   Blaise Pascal, *Pensées* (London: Penguin, 2003), no. 379.

Jesus did many other miraculous signs in the presence of his disciples, which are not recorded in this book. But these are written that you may believe that Jesus is the Christ, the Son of God, and that by believing you may have life in his name. (John 20:30-31)

3 / MESSENGER

The Bible was 'put together by crude, uncultured human mammals'.

Christopher Hitchens[1]

Jesus' teaching is not the product of human learning, of whatever kind. It originates from immediate contact with the Father, from 'face-to-face' dialogue – from the vision of the one who rests close to the Father's heart. It is the Son's word.

Pope Benedict XVI[2]

Dear J,

Sorry about the wee prayer at the end of the last letter. You do understand that it is only because I care for you that, at times, I can be a bit earnest in trying to persuade you to

---

1. Christopher Hitchens, *God Is Not Great* (London: Atlantic Books, 2007), p. 102.

2. Pope Benedict XVI, *Jesus of Nazareth: From the Baptism in the Jordan to the Transfiguration* (London: Bloomsbury Publishing, 2008), p. 7.

accept Jesus Christ. Forgive me. I honestly don't expect you to believe things because I do, or because I say some things passionately. My hope is that you would be able to think these things through for yourself. I was greatly struck by reading the following in the life of Traudl Junge, Hitler's secretary:

> A life of conscious thought began for me only after the war, when I started thinking about important things, asking questions. Wondering about the meaning of human relationships. Until then I'd just accepted everything as it happened to me. I moved from place to place without consciously wanting to leave my mark on them. Wherever I was, I just tried to take an interest in what I was doing, and give of my best.[3]

When it comes to the big questions, sadly there are far too many people who are agnostic and just do their best to avoid thinking. I am delighted that you are not in that category and that you are taking time to think through these things.

I don't expect to have one knock-down argument that will cause you to become a follower of Christ. My case is a cumulative one. Right now, belief in Jesus might look to you like Mount Improbable. But the way we climb Mount Improbable is one step at a time, and that is often the way that God reveals Himself to us. So let's reflect on where we have got to so far. We have seen that Christians believe not

---

3.   Traudl Junge, *Until the Final Hour* (New York: Arcade Publishing, 2004), p. 234.

in a myth, but in a real historical figure who came in space and time, into a particular place at a particular time; that the story of this Jesus was recorded in what we call the Gospels, which purport to be historical documents (and should be judged as such); that there is other historical evidence for Jesus outwith the Bible; that these Gospels claimed that Jesus' conception was a miraculous event; that we should not automatically discount the possibility of miracles, but instead should be open-minded to investigate them; that Jesus did many different miracles to show His identity, kingdom and character; that Christians believe that Jesus can still do miracles today, through His Spirit; and that the greatest miracle is when we come to believe in Him.

Let's now come on to the next step – the message and teaching of Jesus. There is a lot of woolly thinking on this subject. In most of Western culture, people generally have a positive view of Jesus and His message. You will often hear people say something along these lines: 'Jesus is cool/nice/ love but it's the church I don't like' (yet this is the church that Jesus created); 'I love the teachings of Jesus, but I don't like the Bible' (which begs the question how they know what the teachings of Jesus are); and 'I love Jesus and his message, but I don't like the God of the Old Testament' (except they forget that the message of Jesus is that the God of the Old Testament is His Father, and the God of compassion and mercy). They often claim to like the simple teachings of Jesus and yet then misquote them. The fact is that the teaching, the message, of Jesus continues to fascinate. Consider this – Jesus Christ never wrote a book, but thousands of books have been written about him. He never wrote a peer-reviewed research paper, and yet he was wiser than any academic. He never blogged or tweeted and yet has more followers than Justin Bieber or Stephen Fry!

How do we know what the teaching of Jesus is?

Amy Orr-Ewing was asked during her viva voce for her BA whether she was really trying to say that Jesus actually spoke the words recorded in the Gospels, and that the events recorded in the Bible really took place. Her response was to ask the basis on which her questioners assumed that Jesus did not say these words. As in my previous letter, I am quite prepared to defend the view that we know the teaching of Jesus through the Bible. The New Testament Gospels were, after all, written by those who were His companions for three years, who heard His teachings and who went on to spread them. Who better to pass on His teachings? Richard Bauckham, in his book *Jesus and the Eyewitnesses*[4] – a tour de force of New Testament scholarship – offers overwhelming and compelling evidence that the Gospels contain eyewitness testimony, and that the first readers of those Gospels saw them as such.

---

4. Richard Bauckham, *Jesus and the Eyewitnesses: The Gospels as Eyewitness Testimony* (Grand Rapids, Michigan, and Cambridge, U.K.: Eerdmans, 2006).

Some people have real difficulty in accepting any concept of God being able to reveal Himself. It is not a logical difficulty but rather an emotional one. It is deeply prejudiced. I like what Pope Benedict says about this anti-Christian viewpoint:

> And the Antichrist, with an air of scholarly excellence, tells us that any exegesis that reads the Bible from the perspective of faith in the living God, in order to listen to what God has to say, is fundamentalism; he wants to convince us that only his kind of exegesis, the supposedly purely scientific kind, in which God says nothing and has nothing to say, is able to keep abreast of the times.[5]

Spot on. I love what one of my old professors, Donald Macleod, says about this question. He points out that if you dismiss Jesus as the author of the sayings He is recorded as teaching, you end up with an even bigger problem:

> This man who criticises the Apostles, criticises his own culture, who moves so freely among women, who teaches the most splendid parables, who preached the Sermon on the Mount, who prayed the prayer of John 17 – who created him? Which of the Gospel writers had the literary genius? They were unlearned men, unlettered men – which of them created Jesus?[6]

---

5. Pope Benedict XVI, *Jesus of Nazareth,* p. 36.

6. Donald Macleod, *West Highland Free Press.*

Let's just pause for a moment. I need to clarify something which you pointed out before. You have noticed that I have been using the phrases 'the teaching of Jesus', 'the Word of God' and 'the Bible' as interchangeable. Why not have a red-letter Bible, where the actual sayings of Jesus are in red and the rest, especially the Old Testament, can be sidelined as not necessarily being the teaching of Christ? Because Jesus Himself regarded the whole Bible as the Word of God, and as being about Him. After His resurrection, for example, Jesus met two of His disciples and rebuked them for their lack of faith.

> He said to them, 'How foolish you are, and how slow of heart to believe all that the prophets have spoken! Did not the Christ have to suffer these things and then enter his glory?' And beginning with Moses and all the Prophets, he explained to them what was said in all the Scriptures concerning himself.[7]

He clearly believed that the whole Bible spoke of Him.

Jesus grew up like any Jewish boy, learning the Old Testament. The only incident we have of Him as a small boy (aged twelve) is when He went missing and after three days was found in the temple listening to the teachers of the Law (another term for the Word of God) and asking questions of them. He often quoted the Old Testament and declared that

---

7.   Luke 24:25-27.

not a word of it would pass away. In his lovely little book on the Psalms, Dietrich Bonhoeffer points out that the psalms were the prayers and songs that Jesus would have sung. In our church we always sing at least one psalm – not least because it is thrilling to think that these are the songs Jesus sang. At a more personal level, I have always sung or prayed one of these Bible songs every day. During my illness, my family did not know what to pray but the psalms were there and they were ideally suited for our situation. The prayers of Jesus become the prayers of His people.

How did Jesus teach?

The people in Jesus' day were used to hearing religious teachers. I suspect they found them as boring, irrelevant and incomprehensible as we find many today. But He was different. Take this account from Matthew's Gospel: 'When Jesus had finished saying these things, the crowds were amazed at his teaching, because he taught as one who had authority, and not as their teachers of the law.'[8] He taught as one who had authority. He did not pontificate, nor state that rabbi so-and-so says such-and-such, but, on the other hand, this rabbi says this and that. His authority was not the authority of the tyrant, the bully, or the show-off. It was simply the authority of truth, the authority of God. It rang true to the people. And they were amazed.

---

8.   Matthew 7:28-29.

His style was clear, profound and simple. 'Jesus said great things so simply that he seems not to have thought about them, and yet so clearly that it is obvious what he thought about them. Such clarity together with such simplicity is wonderful' (Pascal).[9] Justin Martyr said about Christ's teaching that 'brief and concise utterances fell from Him, for he was no sophist, but His word was the power of God'.[10] Jesus used parables, irony, humour and questions.

How can we understand it today?

Is there a secret to understanding the Bible? Is there a Bible code? Do we need some mystical experience or the insights of some special guru? Are the only people who can understand the Bible those who have a theological degree? I don't think so. My view is quite simple – why not just read it as it is written, trusting that God knew what He was doing when He inspired His Word? That does not mean a literalistic reading: when Jesus said He was the door, He did not mean that He was made of wood and had a handle. John Lennox highlights the difference between literal and literalistic: 'It is therefore common nowadays to reserve the word literalistic for an adherence to the basic primary meaning of a word or

9.   Blaise Pascal, *Pensées* (London: Penguin, 2003), no. 310.

10.   *First Apology of Justin,* in Alexander Roberts, et al (Eds), *The Ante-Nicene Fathers: the Writings of the Fathers Down to A.D. 325, Volume I: The Apostolic Fathers With Justin Martyr and Irenaeus* (New York: Cosimo, Inc., 2007), p. 167.

expression, and literal for the natural reading as intended by the author or speaker.'[11] We should read the Bible as it was written. Sure there are difficult parts, and some things you will keep coming back to. But the great thing about the Bible is that reading it for the first time you can learn so much; reading it for the thousandth time you can still learn so much.

For the most part, the Bible is simple but not simplistic. There is incredible depth. I have been studying the Bible for over thity years and I am still amazed at it. Sometimes, it is depressing for me to go to a church, or to watch a Christian TV programme, and hear teaching that is shallow, superficial and as useless as a chocolate teapot. Somehow, some in the modern church have got it into their heads that the teaching of Jesus is not suitable for our age and that it needs them to make it more relevant. Here is the rub. We don't need to make the Bible relevant – it *is* relevant. What takes a special skill is to make the Bible irrelevant, and yet that is a skill that seems to be acquired quite easily. I suspect that for many people, though, the issue is not so much of not understanding, as of not liking. As Mark Twain famously said, 'It ain't those parts of the Bible that I can't understand that bother me, it's the parts that I do understand!'

---

11. John Lennox, *Seven Days that Divide the World: The Beginning According to Genesis and Science* (Grand Rapids, Michigan: Zondervan, 2011), p. 25.

Some misunderstandings

There are those who try to find inconsistencies in the teaching of Jesus. Our friend Christopher Hitchens tries his best.

> Jesus, it is true, shows no personal interest in gain, but he does speak of treasure in heaven and even of 'mansions' as an inducement to follow him. Is it not further true that all religions down the ages have shown a keen interest in the amassment of material goods in the real world?[12]

I am sure you can effortlessly see where Hitchens is going wrong. To link the treasures and mansions in heaven to the greed of many religious people is just a cheap rhetorical shot. As it happens, I agree that many people use religion as a justification for greed; as Paul says, they think that godliness is a way to get rich. But that is condemned strongly by Christ and His apostles. Those who use Jesus in that way will find that Judgment Day will not be kind to them!

Just as cheap is Hitchens's attempt to show Jesus as saying things that are bad; for example, when He tries to accuse Jesus of being rude to His mother, Mary: 'Jesus is repeatedly very rude and coarse to her when she makes an appearance.'[13]

Some of the misunderstandings come about because the teachings of Jesus can be radical and appear to be quite

---

12. *God Is Not Great*, p. 158.

13. Ibid, p.116.

hard. There are several of these. I can't deal with them all just now, but if you are interested, there is an old book that I have found really helpful, F. F. Bruce's *Hard Sayings of Jesus*. One example he discusses is that of Jesus apparently telling people to hate their parents:

> Large crowds were travelling with Jesus, and turning to them he said: 'If anyone comes to me and does not hate his father and mother, his wife and children, his brothers and sisters – yes, even his own life – he cannot be my disciple. And anyone who does not carry his cross and follow me cannot be my disciple.[14]

The key in understanding difficult passages is to interpret the Bible with the Bible, and always in context. Jesus taught that those who follow Him should honour their parents. So what did He mean? He was talking to large crowds that were following Him because of His miracles. He wanted to warn them that following Him was not going to be easy; that they could not even let family ties prevent them from following Him. He was not telling us to hate our families. His language was shocking, arresting and challenging. It still is.

Some people get confused about the teaching of Jesus primarily because they just don't believe it, and don't want to believe it, and yet they still want the trappings of religion. There are those who don't really believe that we can know

---

14.   Luke 14:25-27.

the message of Jesus, so, in essence, we can just make it up. I once sat in a room of church leaders who were asked to explain the message of Jesus. It was astounding how some managed to come up with comments like: 'My Jesus was a gay Jesus; my Jesus was a communist Jesus; my Jesus …' I wanted to scream, 'I don't want to hear about *your* Jesus; I want to hear Jesus!' I love what the former Pope Benedict asks: 'Was Jesus in reality a liberal rabbi – a forerunner of Christian liberalism? Is the Christ of faith, and therefore the whole faith of the Church, just one big mistake?' The fact is that those who change (either by adding to, or taking away from) the message of Jesus are destroying it.

Again it is Justin Martyr from the second century who puts it wonderfully, talking about those who attack the teachings of Christ, without really knowing what they are:

> For if he assails us without having read the teachings of Christ, he is thoroughly depraved, and far worse than the illiterate, who often refrain from discussing or bearing false witness about matters they do not understand. Or, if he has read them and does not understand the majesty that is in them, or, understanding it, acts that he may not be suspected of being such a Christian, he is far more base and thoroughly depraved, being conquered by illiberal and unreasonable opinion and fear.[15]

---

15.   Justin Martyr, *Second Apology*, in Alexander Roberts, et al (Eds), *The Ante-Nicene Fathers, Volume I*, p. 189

What is the message?

Let me say first of all what it is not. The message is not moralism, nor legalism. The religious Pharisee does not need God at all. He makes himself righteous. The liberal version of that is also a kind of self-righteousness. This is the kind of teaching which sees God as some kind of Daddy in the sky who tells us all how to behave ourselves and rewards us with sweeties. It is the notion of God that many grow up with and not surprisingly reject. It has been described as 'moralistic, therapeutic deism'.

Nor is the message of Jesus something that is lost and needs to be rediscovered by some aspiring theologian or prophet. In this respect, please beware of people who come declaring that they have discovered 'The lost message of Jesus'. You asked about the book bearing that title by a well-known English evangelical called Steve Chalke. Well, it is well written and contains many things that it would be hard to disagree with but, as for its main premise, I'm afraid there is nothing new about it. It is a rehash of nineteenth-century Protestant liberalism in the guise of twenty-first century evangelicalism. Let me give you some examples of how this works. Chalke tells the story of a child who declared that the message of Jesus was that of Dr Spock from *Star Trek*, 'Live long and prosper.' I think that if you actually read the teaching of Jesus you will find there might be a little bit more to it than that! Then there is the hubristic statement that the church has not really understood the message of Jesus (until twenty-first century theologians with books to sell came along to enlighten us!): 'For us the realisation that God is love has taken a long time to sink in. In fact it has taken two millennia for the penny finally to drop.'[16] And finally, there is the Disneyesque, positive-thinking sound bite, geared precisely for our self-obsessed society: 'Jesus' message is not do I believe in God, but does God believe in me – to which Jesus' answer is yes.' I'm sorry, but such twee guff makes me feel ill – it is so far away from the message of Jesus, who, in this respect, simply declares that the work God requires is 'to believe in the one he has sent' (John 6:29).

But now I have a problem. I cannot really summarize the message of Jesus in a few words. I would simply suggest that you read His message for yourself. Read the Gospels, the letters, the prophets, the poetical books, the law and the histories. They all speak of Christ.

If I *had* to summarize, I would say that although Jesus taught about many things – money, sex, God, humanity – the best summary is His own. He said that He had come to teach about the kingdom of God: 'I must preach the good news of the kingdom of God to the other towns also, because that is why I was sent.'[17]. Of course, there have been millions

---

16. Steve Chalke, *The Lost Message of Jesus* (Grand Rapids, Michigan: Zondervan, 2004), p. 46.

17. Luke 4:43.

of words written about what this means, but I like the simple and best understanding that the kingdom of God is where God's reign as King is honoured and His will is done. It is a kingdom of joy, peace, justice and righteousness. It is good news (hence the term, 'gospel') because it is a kingdom of love. This is what really gets Hitchens: 'The order to love thy neighbour as thyself is too extreme and too strenuous to be obeyed, as is the hard to interpret instruction to "love others as I have loved you"! Humans are not so constituted as to care for others as much as themselves: the thing simply cannot be done'.[18] Hitchens thinks that the Christian command to love our enemies, or to love others as we love ourselves, is absurd because it is impossible. I agree. It is too extreme and strenuous, unless we grasp that this is what Christ did and what He empowers us to do. It is one of those miracles that Hitchens denies. Bertrand Russell puts it better: 'Nothing can penetrate the loneliness of the human heart except the highest intensity of the sort of love the religious teachers have produced.'[19] And peerless amongst those teachers was the one who is Love Himself.

The message of the kingdom is the message of the King – it is about Jesus Himself. That is why it is good news. If you or I taught a message which was about us then we

---

18. Christopher Hitchens, *God Is Not Great*, p. 213.

19. Cited in Antony Flew, *There is a God* (New York: HarperCollins, 2008), p. xxi.

would rightly be accused of arrogance and conceit. But Jesus taught about Himself because He really is the good news. His message is one of self-witness. His use of the terms Son of Man and the Son of David were in the context of the Old Testament claims to Deity. He was claiming He was God. He claimed to be able to forgive sins (Matt. 9:6) and to be the Son of God (Matt. 28:19). His teaching comes not from human learning, which is always derivative, but from direct contact with God the Father. That is what makes it so authoritative and powerful.

Does Jesus still speak today?

I wonder what you would do if someone told you that Jesus was speaking to them? Suggest they get psychiatric help? Please don't think that when we talk about Jesus speaking today we are talking primarily about visions and voices. I don't dispute that God can use these things but I do dispute that that is how He normally communicates with us.

I think He does still speak, but through His Word. 'And let us not take into our heads either to seek out God anywhere else than in his Sacred Word, or to think anything about him that is not prompted by his Word, or to speak anything that is not taken from that Word.'[20]

This is so vital. Remember how in the last letter we talked about how you might say you would believe if you

---

20. John Calvin, *Institutes of the Christian Religion*, 1:21.

saw a miracle; and yet, although miracles are signs, we need something more certain and more sure. The answer is that we have that in Christ and His Word. 'If people do not believe the word of Scripture, then they will not believe someone coming from the next world either. The highest truths cannot be forced into the type of empirical evidence that only applies to material reality.'[21] Some people want to accuse those of us who believe this of reducing the person of Christ into a book. They talk about how the Word became flesh and the church has now made Him Word again. But they are making a false dichotomy between 'logos' (reason, the impartation of information) and reality. In the Bible, God spoke and the world came into being. He sends His Son to speak life into us. The Word still speaks life into us. The law has become a person, Jesus Christ, who is Himself the Truth – and He communicates Himself through truth. To set Jesus up against the Bible is one of the most successful lies of the devil. 'I don't believe in a book, I trust in a person' sounds neat until you ask whether you trust the book that the person gave! That is why He chose His twelve disciples and gave them the Holy Spirit, so that they could remember, record, proclaim and pass on His teaching.

One of the dubious perks of being a minister is that every now and then someone jokes about how you only work one

---

21.   Pope Benedict XVI, *Jesus of Nazareth*, p. 216..

day per week. One middle-aged man wanted to push the joke further and asked, 'Would you go to church twice on a Sunday if you weren't paid to do so?' When I answered 'Yes', knowing that I was a football fan, he asked, 'If you were given the opportunity of watching Rangers in a cup final or going to church, which one would you choose?' 'I would prefer to hear the Word of God.' 'You fanatic!' (The irony of this coming from a man who spent a fortune every weekend travelling to watch eleven grown men kick a pig's bladder around a field!) I don't think it is fanatical at all. The Word of God is my spiritual milk, bread and meat. I could no more survive without it than I could without literal milk, bread and meat. I love hearing it being proclaimed, I love proclaiming it. Jesus still speaks.

Before I leave you, let me remind you of how important this is. Words are powerful but they are rarely permanent – except for the words of Christ. He says, 'Heaven and earth will pass away, but my words will never pass away.'[22] That's how important the teaching of Jesus is. It's why you really need to get to know it. Whilst I was in hospital, one of the nurses was keen to shower me (I know – too much information!). I wondered why, but it became apparent that she wanted to talk away from the public space of the ward. She asked about how we could read and understand

---

22.   Matthew 24:35.

the Bible. She told me that she had tried to read the Bible but did not think she could understand it. The same advice I gave to her I now offer to you. Firstly, it is important to read the Bible, but not just by yourself. Read it in community, where others can share your questions and you can explore it together. Either a church study group or a course like *Christianity Explored* can be really helpful. Secondly, make sure you have a good, accurate, modern translation of the Bible (write for advice if you want some!). In addition, it's probably not good to begin with Genesis and work your way through the whole sixty-six books systematically. Try the Gospel of Mark, followed by Ecclesiastes, Ephesians, Psalms, Genesis, and from there on. Mix and match the different genres of Scripture (poetry, Gospel, letters, history, prophets). Thirdly, I really do recommend that you get some good Bible-teaching. Go to a church and listen to what is proclaimed (but always keep your wits about you – avoid churches which seem to ignore or sideline the Bible, and be wary of those who are legalistic, adding to it, or liberal, taking away from it). Again, I am happy to help you with churches in your area. It is not the denomination that matters so much as the faithfulness to the Word of God. Finally, we are back to prayer. It is the Spirit who makes the reading and the preaching of the Word effective in our hearts and minds. I will pray for you, but why don't you pray for yourself? Use the words of the Psalmist that I will leave at the end of this letter. In my next letter, we will move on to the most difficult and hard-to-accept part of the whole of Jesus' teaching – the cross. Take care.

Yours etc.,

David

> Open my eyes that I may see wonderful things in your law.[23] (Note that *law* is another word the Bible uses for itself.)

---

23. Ps. 119:18.

4 / MURDERED

Once again we have a father demonstrating love by subjecting a son to death by torture, but this time the father is not trying to impress god. He is god, and he is trying to impress humans.

Christopher Hitchens, *God is not Great*[1]

... unless for him
Some other able, and as willing, pay
The rigid satisfaction, death for death.
Say heavenly powers, where shall we find such love,
Which of ye will be mortal to redeem
Man's mortal crime, and just the unjust to save,
Dwells in all heaven charity so dear?

John Milton, *Paradise Lost*[2]

Dear J.

Thanks for the letter and the questions within. I'll try to cover most of them but there is one that we need to address right away, because it is a question that causes great confusion. You ask why Christians are so divided

---

1. Christopher Hitchens, *God Is Not Great* (London: Atlantic Books, 2007), p. 209.

2. John Milton, *Paradise Lost*, III:210–16.

about what the teaching of Jesus actually is. Why are there so many disputes that I criticized in my last letter? Isn't it just everyone making up a Jesus in their own image? It's a great question, and one that really confuses many within and outwith the church. Grant the existence of the devil for a moment, and think about what his best tactic would be to limit the spread of the message of Jesus. Surely it would be to deny either that there was such a message, or to imply that even if there was, we could not really know it. The best way to do that is to get those who profess to be the proclaimers of that message to send out different messages. And in many ways he succeeds. The thing that puts me off Christianity more than anything is the false teaching that goes around in Christ's name (I won't bore you with examples, but feel free to ask!). I realize, of course, that you can then charge me with arrogance for implying that I alone (or people who think like me) have 'the truth' and that we are the kind of people who want to go round burning heretics. But allow me to deny the charge. I don't think I alone have the truth, I think Christ is the truth and I must seek truth in Him. Many times I can get it wrong (and that is why I ask you not to believe me, but to believe Him). It really makes sense that He would reveal Himself in His Word because, if that is not the case, you are then reduced to either expecting direct, personal, divine revelation, or relying on different human messengers to be infallible prophets. The bottom line is that when the church has moved away from the Bible as the complete and clear Word of God, it has moved away from Christ. That is how we end up with cults like the Jehovah's Witnesses and the Mormons, whose founders just did not like some of the things they read in the Bible and so changed it, all the while claiming new 'divine revelation'. Or, on the other hand, we see dead and dying churches, whose leaders have forgotten that the Bible is supposed to be the message of Christ, not the church's message adapted and suited to what they think their culture is, or should be. I know this is difficult to accept, but surely an almighty God is able to reveal Himself to us in such a way that His message is never lost, and always true. This is not to say that Christians will always agree on everything. The Bible is not a simple book, and there are issues where more than one interpretation is equally valid. On top of that we are sinful, so, of course, there will be ongoing learning, growth and development. But the truth is that God's Word is true, and on that basis we can work out everything else. It is not the other way round – that we are true and reasonable, and on that basis can work out whether God's Word is true.

Before we move on to the next step in your search, permit me to recap the story of Jesus so far. He was born over two thousand years ago in Palestine, during the time of the Roman occupation of Israel. His birth was miraculous. His life was ordinary until the age of thirty (working as a carpenter, looking after his mother after his father had died). Aged thirty, he began his ministry by being baptized by John the Baptist, and for three years he taught about the kingdom of God, evidencing it with some extraordinary miracles. Then he was murdered. End of story. Not!

I hope you took my advice to read the Gospels. If you did, you will have noticed something strange, at least to modern eyes. They are – to say the least – unusual biographies. They are not directly linear and, most notably, 50 per cent of the content is taken up with the death of their subject – Jesus. This is stranger still when you consider the manner of His death: not a heroic death in a last, mighty battle charge, but a bloody and cruel end, treated as a criminal in dishonour and disgrace. If you think the teaching of Jesus is sometimes difficult, His teaching about the cross and what the Bible says about it, has proved more divisive and difficult. It really is very hard for modern minds to grasp. But not just 'modern minds'! The apostle Paul tells us:

> Jews demand miraculous signs and Greeks look for wisdom, but we preach Christ crucified: a stumbling block to Jews and foolishness to Gentiles, but to those whom God has called, both Jews and Greeks, Christ the power of God and the wisdom of God. For the foolishness of God is wiser than man's wisdom, and the weakness of God is stronger than man's strength.[3]

---

3.   1 Corinthians 1:22-25.

Certainly, to many (and perhaps to you?) the cross appears foolish.

As evidenced by the quote at the start of this letter, Hitchens certainly thinks so. His friend Richard Dawkins agrees it is barking mad. And many people who are not card-carrying anti-theists find the whole idea of the atonement somewhat disgusting. Even many professing Christians shy away from the biblical teaching on this, and feel more than a little embarrassed by it. So rather than being squeamish and turning away, let's see if we can advance our understanding of who Jesus is, by looking at His death. He said Himself that if people wanted to get what He was about, they had to accept that He came to die. It is therefore clear that we can't hope to understand Him unless we can tackle this head-on.

What happened?
I am not going to repeat again the reasons why we can trust the Gospel accounts, but I thought you might appreciate this anecdote told by Pope Benedict about the Anglican, C. S. Lewis: 'Once Lewis overheard a firm atheist remarking to a colleague that the evidence for the historicity of the Gospels was actually surprisingly good. The atheist then paused thoughtfully and said: "About the dying God. Rum thing. It almost looks as if it really happened once."'[4]

---

4. Pope Benedict XVI, *Jesus of Nazareth: From the Baptism in the Jordan to the Transfiguration* (London: Bloomsbury Publishing, 2008), p. 271.

In or around the year A.D. 30, Jesus went to Jerusalem and, after a few days, was arrested by the Jewish leaders and brought before the Roman Governor, Pontius Pilate. Although Pilate found no case against Him, he agreed to crucify Jesus, releasing the murderer Barabbas instead (apparently a tradition like a presidential pardon). Christ was crucified, together with two thieves, on the hill of the skull (called Golgotha or Calvary), just outside the city wall. I don't really want to go into all the details because it really is horrendous. On this I completely agree with Hitchens. Suffice it to say that crucifixion was a Roman punishment that could best be described as death by torture. After being beaten and tortured, the victims were forced to carry their own cross to the execution site and then had their hands and feet nailed to the crossbeam and upright. There were different types of cross for different forms of execution. The Roman one was made of wood with a vertical stake and a horizontal plank. Because of Christianity it is now the most recognized symbol in the world (in a recent poll, beating the McDonald's sign and the Coca-Cola symbol in terms of 'brand recognition'). It is not without significance that the Jews did not use crucifixion, because they regarded it as a death cursed by God (Deut. 21:23). Usually the victim would be offered a mixture of vinegar, gall and myrrh (some kind of narcotic for pain relief), and sometimes support was given (wooden footrests, for example, being nailed to the cross). The latter was not out of mercy but in order to prolong the agony. The only way to breathe was to press upward on nail-pierced feet to open the lungs for breath. Death could take up to three days. If the victim was not supported, then hanging from nail-pierced wrists would lead to exhaustion, suffocation, brain death and heart failure. Sometimes, breaking the victims' legs would speed up the procedure. Often the charges against the victim would be placed above their heads, as the execution was always held in a very public place.

Does it not depress you that human beings can invent such diabolical methods of treating one another? And that there would be crowds who, with a ghoulish fascination, would come to watch this gore-fest? I remember the first time I saw Mel Gibson's *The Passion of the Christ,* how ill I felt – I left the cinema with a migraine. Incidentally, the value of Gibson's film was that it did give some idea of the horror of the cross, and in doing so helped mitigate the ridiculous image that many people have of a serenely smiling Jesus looking down and blessing the world. Monty Python were, of course, blasphemous in their depiction of the Christ-like figure singing, 'Always look on the bright side of life', but I'm not sure they were in that respect worse than mental images of crucifixion that some Christians have. The reality is, though, that the cross was actually far worse for Jesus than Gibson's film could communicate, because he wasn't able to portray the spiritual suffering and sin-bearing of Christ. The cross is so horrific that I struggle with the idea of it being turned into bling jewellery, or even being used as a symbol of any kind. What would you think of someone who wore a gold chain with the gates of Auschwitz as its centrepiece? That is the horror of the cross. It is the sum of all our infinite hells rolled into one moment of time and placed on one man. *Why?*

Why did He die?

Christopher Hitchens sees it as some kind of attempt by God to impress human beings. That really is one of his sillier 'straw man' arguments. No Christian argues that and the Bible does not teach it.

The trouble is that Hitchens just doesn't get the idea of forgiveness and atonement. Like many people, he thinks Christianity is about obeying God's rules and thus qualifying for heaven: 'Imagine, further, that if you obey the rules and commandments that he has lovingly prescribed, you will qualify for an eternity of bliss and repose.'[5] Likewise, John Humphrys just doesn't get it. 'Don't worry about death because if you are good you'll go to heaven.'[6] Please let me repeat over and over again that the good news is NOT that if you are good you will get to heaven. In fact, the good news is

---

5.   Christopher Hitchens, *God Is Not Great*, p. 15.

6.   John Humphrys, *In God We Doubt* (London: Hodder and Stoughton, 2007), p. 25.

that you can never be good enough to get to heaven. Which doesn't sound like good news until you see the cross. It is at the cross that God deals with our badness, ugliness and rebellion against Him, and gives us His goodness, beauty and purity – in the greatest and best swap of all time.

The Bible does teach that Christ died and suffered in this horrendous way because He was suffering in our place. That is where the problem lies for some. For example, a minister in my own home city wrote in his congregational newsletter that the atonement (the technical term for this swap) is barbaric and not Christian at all. You may be inclined to agree. And you would find some other professing Christians who would go along with you (remember what we discussed about the devil undermining the clear message of Christ by getting 'Christian' teachers to muddy the waters?). Steve Chalke, for example, in the book I mentioned in my last letter, said this: 'The fact is that the cross isn't a form of cosmic child abuse – a vengeful Father, punishing his Son for an offence he has not committed. Understandably both people inside and outside the church have found this twisted version of events morally dubious and a high barrier to faith.'[7] Actually, the cross is highly offensive and a great barrier to faith. But it is not faith for its own sake that we are interested in, nor what proves attractive to people. We

---

7.   Steve Chalke, *The Lost Message of Jesus* (Grand Rapids, Michigan: Zondervan, 2004), p. 102.

are interested in searching for what is true. Let me offer you an alternative explanation that shows why the cross is truly wonderful.

It's all to do with this word 'atonement'. Ian McEwan wrote a superb book of the same name. In one sense, his book is not about the Bible's idea of atonement at all; McEwan is an atheist and the book is a novel, but it does explore the theme with quite extraordinary beauty. The main character in the story commits a terrible sin which has dreadful consequences for lots of people. The rest of her life is spent seeking to make amends or 'atone' for that one lie. 'There is no one, no entity or higher form that she can appeal to, or be reconciled with, or that can forgive her. There is nothing outside her. In her imagination she has set the limits and terms.'[8] But the poignant message of the book is really that atonement proves impossible.

Take the dictionary definition of the word.

1. Reparation for a wrong or injury: 'she wanted to make atonement for her behaviour'.

2. Reparation or expiation for sin.

That just about sums it up. We do wrong; we cause injury. We, in the Bible's word, commit 'sin'. Sin is a word that people dislike and too often associate with sex, but it is

8.   Ian McEwan, *Atonement* (London: Vintage, 2007), p. 371.

a deep and profound word, and we really do need to grasp it. It expresses the idea not just of doing the evil we should not do, but also of failing to do the good we should do – sins of commission and omission. Just as we recognize the concept of justice in our society (you do the crime, you pay the time) so there is a deep-seated justice within the universe created by God. There is an ultimate Judge to whom we will answer for all our sins – that is both scary and wonderful. After all, who would want to live in a universe where there was no justice, and people got away with evil?

But you might want to argue that, whilst you are not perfect, you have done nothing that deserves any real punishment. Like the French philosopher Rousseau, you want to believe that 'God will forgive me, that's his job'! Can I dare to suggest that I think this is your perspective, and that as such it is an entirely emotional rather than a rational one? What if we take a starting point other than your feelings, or mine for that matter, or the standards of the culture around us? What if we start with the cross? Could it be that the need for atonement is real, and that what is in us is so deep, and so ingrained, that only the most radical surgery could deal with it?

We like to think that people who commit what we call inhuman acts are not human. One of the great revelatory moments in my life was when I came to realize that Adolf Hitler and the Nazis were human, just like me; that I could have gone down the same route; that the same principle of evil in them was also in me. Those who live in the Disneyesque, modernist fantasy world of post-enlightenment liberalism do like to keep telling themselves that human beings are basically good and getting better. It's what we mean by 'progressive'. But does the evidence bear that out? What if that is not true? What if our prints are all over the 'smoking gun'? What if there is evil out there? Even worse, what if there is evil within me? 'If only it were all so simple! If only there were evil people somewhere insidiously committing evil deeds, and it were necessary only to separate them from the rest of us and destroy them. But the line dividing good and evil cuts through the heart of every human being. And who is willing to destroy a piece of his own heart?' (Solzhenitsyn).[9] How can that be dealt with? For those who disagree I offer a simple experiment – see if you can go one whole week without saying, doing or thinking anything bad. Why do we find that impossible?

If we are sinners, who is going to pay for our sin? The Bible says that we can – if we wish. But that is what hell is. I realize, at this point, that to go into the whole teaching about and objections to hell would make this letter the length of *War and Peace*. But let me ask you to at least accept the logic of this thought: if heaven is where God is in all

---

9.   Aleksandr Solzhenitsyn, *The Gulag Archipelago 1918-1956*.

His mercy, grace and love, and hell is where God is not, then surely those who choose to live without God are simply getting what they requested? Jesus came to save us from the hell of our sins, the hell we choose to go to ourselves when we shake our fist at God and say, 'No, I want to have it my way!' Jesus suffered hell so that we don't have to.

When Jesus went to the cross, He was forsaken – not just by His people, His enemies, and His friends and family. He was forsaken by God His Father. He became the sin-bearer, and the punishment that brought us peace was laid upon Him. He paid the price, carried the load and bore our hell. It was such a moment of intense pain that on His way to the cross, when He was in the Garden of Gethsemane, He prayed, 'My Father, if it is possible, may this cup be taken from me. Yet not as I will, but as you will.'[10] In fact, it was so intense that we are told His soul was overwhelmed almost to the point of death. On the cross, He quoted one of the songs He would have learned in His youth – a song which was a prophecy about that very moment He was enduring, Psalm 22: 'My God, my God, why have you forsaken me?' He didn't just quote; he gave a loud cry. He experienced that forsakenness. For that one moment in time, it was as though the Trinity were split. The Son did not feel the love of the Father; He felt the full force of His anger and judgment

---

10.   Matthew 26:39.

against sin. He was forsaken, so that we would never need to be.

Jesus saw His death in these terms: 'This is my body broken for you. This is my blood poured out for many for the remission of sins.' He is the Lamb of God who takes away the sin of the world. It is impossible to be a Christian, a follower of Christ, without this. Without the atonement there is no forgiveness of sins; with the atonement there is. Unlike the death of any wise man, guru, religious founder or hero in the history of mankind, Jesus' death is where the story begins, not where it ends. The atonement is about reconciliation: God was in Christ, reconciling the world to Himself. It is about new life, where there is peace with God and with others.

> Enmity with God is the source of all that poisons man; overcoming this enmity is the basic condition for peace in the world. Only the man who is reconciled with God can also be reconciled and in harmony with himself, and only the man who is reconciled with God and with himself can establish peace around him and throughout the world.[11]

How does it work?

I love the imagery in John Bunyan's classic tale, *The Pilgrim's Progress.*

---

11. Pope Benedict XVI, *Jesus of Nazareth* (2008), p. 85.

And I saw one, as I thought in my mind, hang bleeding upon the tree; and the very sight of him made my burden fall off my back (for I groaned under a heavy burden) but then it fell down from off me. It was a strange thing to me, for I never saw such a thing before; yea, and while I stood looking up, for then I could not forbear looking, three Shining Ones came to me. One of them testified that my sins were forgiven me; another stripped me of my rags, and gave this broidered coat which you see; and the third set the mark which you see in my forehead, and gave me this sealed roll.[12]

That is how it works. You look to Jesus on the cross, confess your sin and admit you cannot deal with it. You accept what He has done, and He takes your burden. He takes the filthy rags of your own good/bad deeds, your own righteousness, your own religion, and He gives you His purity, perfection and relationship with the Father. Then He seals you with His Holy Spirit, so that you will never be lost again.

It all works by looking to Christ, and by humility. Calvin grasped this:

Although the preaching of the cross does not agree with our human inclination, if we desire to return to God our Author and Maker, from whom we have been estranged, in order that he may again begin to be our Father, we ought nevertheless to embrace it humbly.[13]

---

12. John Bunyan, *The Pilgrim's Progress*.

13. John Calvin, *Institutes of the Christian Religion,* 2:6:1.

There is a natural (and sinful) inclination within us which resists the notion that there is nothing we can bring or contribute. We like to think we can strike a deal with God; that there is something that we can do to set matters straight (like Bryony in McEwan's *Atonement*). But we just don't realize how insane it is to try to work our way back into God's favour by good behaviour. Indeed, we are so hard-wired into this assumption that we end up making matters infinitely worse! Such attempts mean that earning God's favour is something we want to be able to boast about, and that is pretty much the definition of pride. So we end up unwittingly attempting to pay for our past sins with a sin! As someone said, 'The thing that separates us from God is not so much our sins as our damnable good works.' The message of the cross is not only that there is nothing you can do to oblige God to accept you, but nothing you need to do. It's all been done. But we have to have the humility to accept it, and luxuriate in it.

The cross works by proving the love of God for us. In a fascinating interview, the writer Douglas Coupland, when asked, 'What is your greatest fear?' expressed his greatest concern: 'That God exists but doesn't care very much for humans.' The cross proves He does. It is while we were still enemies that Christ died for us. We can only love Him because He first loved us. A woman at a bookstore event once asked me during a question-and-answer session, 'You say that God loves you; how can you possibly know that?' It was a great question, possibly the most important question anyone can ever ask. As I answered by explaining what I have just explained to you, her eyes grew wider and wider, and her mouth dropped open. At the end she responded, 'If that is true – and I'm not saying I believe it is – but if it is true, then it is the most wonderful thing I have ever heard.' She got the cross.

You become a Christian through the cross, but one of the wonderful things about being a Christian is that you never move beyond it. The wonder of it just hits you again and again. I love P. T. Forsyth's reflection on the cross. 'There is no new insight into the Cross which does not bring, whatever else come with it, a deeper sense of the solemn holiness of the love that meets us there.'[14]

I often reflect on Paul's words to the Galatians: '... the Son of God who loved me and gave himself for me.'[15] I take the phrase, 'You did that for me,' and place the emphasis on different words. '*You* did that for me' makes me wonder at the glory and beauty of Jesus. 'You did *that* for me' makes me think of what He actually suffered, and causes me to weep for my sin. And 'You did that for *me*' humbles me, and encourages me that the Son of God did indeed love me and give Himself for me.

---

14. P. T. Forsyth. *The Soul of Prayer* (1916), chapter VI.

15. Galatians 2:20.

Where are safe and firm rest and security for the weak but in the Saviour's wounds? The mightier he is to save, the more securely I dwell there. The world menaces, the body weighs us down, the devil sets his snares. I fall not, for I am grounded upon firm rock. I have sinned a grave sin. My conscience is disturbed, but it will not be perturbed because I shall remember the Lord's wounds (Bernard of Clairvaux).[16]

That is why the Gospel writers are keen to show us that the cross is not just about Jesus taking our guilt but that, in so doing, He is taking away the source of our death and granting us life.

Take care,

David

For even the Son of Man did not come to be served, but to serve, and to give his life as a ransom for many (Mark 10:45).

---

16. Cited in John Calvin, *Institutes of the Christian Religion*, 3:12:3.

5 / MARVELLOUS

Our Lord has written the promise of the resurrection not in words alone, but in every leaf in springtime.

Martin Luther

Today, I would say the claim concerning the resurrection is more impressive than any by the religious competition.

Antony Flew[1]

Dear J,

Once again thanks for your responses. It's good to know that you are thinking about these things and have so many questions. I am sorry for raising the thorny issue of hell in the last letter, but if you don't mind I will leave your questions on that one until later. There are, however, two

1.   Antony Flew, *There is a God* (New York: HarperCollins, 2008), p. 187.

issues which you raise which need to be addressed before we move on to the next step.

The first concerns my use of the word 'sin'. I realize, as a concept, this requires a real paradigm shift on your part. You write: 'David, you have such a pessimistic view of human beings that you make Leonard Cohen look optimistic! Your view that all people are "sinners" is so depressing. I have to believe that people are basically good.' Thanks for your honesty. I accept that is what you believe but dare I point out that you are making a faith statement based upon very little evidence? My position sounds worse than you suggest because I believe in something called 'total depravity'. That is, I believe what the Bible teaches – that every single human being is affected and infected in every part of his or her being by sin. It is not that we are as bad as we can be – there is always room for further deterioration – nor that there is no good in us (there are aspects of the image of God in us which allow us both to do and experience extraordinary beauty and goodness). Rather, there are no areas of our individual or collective lives which are not spoiled and tainted by the ugliness of sin. That is what I believe, and I would dare to suggest that I have evidence for this position.

I was asked to prove this once at a meeting held in a bookshop by a secular humanist, who said, like you, 'I *have* to believe in human goodness.' My answer was simple – 'Go to the history section of this bookshop, pick out any book you like, and I will show you proof of humanity's inhumanity.' And it's not just in history. I can pick up any newspaper, watch the news, or consider my own experience and look deep within. At the end of the day, the evidence of human sinfulness is so overwhelming that it takes a special kind of blindness to be able to ignore it!

The good news can be summarized in this way. You are far worse than you think you are, and you are more loved than you ever imagined you could be. Jesus came to show us both.

The second question is really more to do with the purpose of these letters. You ask about my providing 'proof' for many of the statements that I've made. To be honest, I can't. That is not the purpose of these letters. How does one prove a statement such as, 'Jesus died for our sins'? There is no lab test, no video of Jesus being born of a virgin and no telex from heaven giving us all the proof. But it is very important that you realize the difference between evidence and proof. There is plenty of *evidence* for what I assert. I can't list it. Whole books have been written on subjects that I cover in a couple of sentences! However, where we've discussed questions you want to probe for yourself, then what I have done is to seek to point you to the evidence. That's why I mention so many books – not that I expect you to read them all, but so that you can follow up for yourself any particular inquiries you may have. Having said that, there is one subject which I think lends itself to proof – or at least sufficient evidence such that the only reasonable position is to accept it. Would it surprise you if I said that one thing is the resurrection of Jesus Christ?

Before coming to that, let's again mark the signposts on the road we have travelled so far. Jesus Christ was born of the Virgin Mary; He began His 'ministry' aged 30 and, after three years of teaching and miracles, was crucified by the Jewish and Roman authorities (for no civil or criminal crime, but charged with blasphemy). End of story ... except it wasn't. We saw in my last letter that the Bible teaches that Jesus died for a purpose: to carry our sins, and to get and give forgiveness for us if we'll have it. At this point, the whole question of the divinity of Jesus inescapably arises. The pivotal proof for this is His rising from the dead – His resurrection. This is so crucial that I was kind of hoping that this is where we would start. After all, when you read through the book of Acts, you will find that the early disciples often began with the resurrection when they proclaimed the good news. Augustine said of the early disciples that 'the leading truth they professed is that Christ rose from the dead, and first showed in His own flesh the immortality of the resurrection which He promised should be ours.'[2] It is

---

2.   St. Augustine, *City of God and Christian Doctrine: Nicene and Post-Nicene Fathers of the Christian Church*, Part 2, (Whitefish, MT: Kessinger Publishing, 2004), p. 492.

the ultimate game-changer. If the resurrection is true, then everything has changed. As Jaroslav Pelikan once said, 'If Jesus Christ rose from the dead, nothing else matters. If Jesus Christ did not rise from the dead, nothing else matters.'

It is for this reason that the notion of resurrection is so mocked and attacked. Please don't fall for the 'zombie Jesus' routine that some of our atheist comedians think is so amusing and insightful! At the Edinburgh Book Festival in 2009, Christopher Hitchens debated with one of my mentors, John Lennox. John was always well prepared and we discussed some of the tactics and arguments that might be used beforehand. One suggestion was that he simply mention the resurrection as a fact, and watch what happened. In my experience, this is usually like lighting the blue touchpaper: standing back and waiting for the inevitable explosion! Sure enough, in concluding his speech Lennox mentioned the fact of the resurrection of Jesus! The moderator, John Humphrys, asked Hitchens to respond, indicating that he had five minutes. Hitchens barked, 'I won't need five minutes to respond to someone who believes in the resurrection.' This is a standard tactic – equate people who believe in the resurrection with those who believe in a flat earth, Santa Claus and Scotland winning the World Cup, and you then don't need to even think about, never mind examine, the evidence. Again, I am grateful that you are a little more open-minded than that!

The main objection to the resurrection is simple. Resurrections just don't happen. But you need to pause there. I agree. Totally. That is the point. Resurrections *don't* happen. If they did, then the resurrection of Jesus would be no big deal. It would be a bit like me saying, 'Jesus is the Son of God because he recovered from illness.' Getting better is common; getting resurrected is not. In the normal course of events, resurrections don't happen. But the Bible is claiming that this is not the normal course of events; it is the ultimate extraordinary event. So instead of dismissing it we need to ask, 'What happened?' and 'What proof is there?' and then go on to consider the implications.

What happened?

Jesus died. This is important for those who want to argue the 'swoon' theory. This has been suggested at various points in history and is still favoured by some desperate to avoid the evidence for the resurrection. The myth is that Jesus didn't die, but nobody noticed. He was flogged, nailed to a cross for hours, stabbed in the side, covered in spices, wrapped in a shroud. But he revived, neatly folded up the grave clothes (a tidy tomb room is essential because 'cleanliness is next to godliness'!), rolled the stone away, overcame the Roman guards and walked away. Not very likely is it? One of the details in the Gospels is that the Roman soldiers did not break His legs because they saw He was already dead. These were men who had witnessed many executions and deaths, and were fully aware of when someone had died. Is it likely that Jesus fooled them by going into some kind of comatose state and then revived Himself?

He was buried. After His death on the cross, a rich man called Joseph of Arimathea, aided by the Pharisee, Nicodemeus, took the body of Jesus to his own cave tomb. This was a family tomb that would have been used for the burial of wealthy people. They left the body there after sealing the tomb with a massive rock. The women who followed Jesus were watching from a distance because they wanted to follow the Jewish practice of dressing the body. But they did not do so immediately because night fell, and it was then the Sabbath. They determined to return on the Sunday to do the job. Meanwhile, the Jewish Sanhedrin (a kind of religious court) asked the Roman governor Pilate to put a guard on the tomb, which was then sealed.

On the Sunday, the first day of the week, the women (including Mary Magdalene, Joanna and Mary, the mother of James) took the spices and went to the tomb, only to find that the stone had been rolled away, and the body was gone. They were told by 'men in clothes that gleamed like lightning' that Jesus was not there and that He had risen, as He had predicted. They told the eleven disciples, who did not believe them. Peter then went to the tomb and saw the evidence of the grave clothes with no body in them. In the differing accounts, we read that Mary spoke to Jesus; that Jesus turned up in a room with the disciples; and that there were then various other resurrection appearances, including at one point to over five hundred at once.

From that point on, it was an essential part of the early Christian church that it consisted of those who believed that Jesus had really risen from the dead. That is the assertion; that is what we believe today. We do not worship a dead Lord, revere an honourable teacher from the past, or seek to keep 'the spirit' of a great leader alive in our midst. When we worship Jesus Christ, we do so to a living being. So then the question becomes: do we have a basis for thinking in such a way?

Prove it!

Firstly, we have the *eyewitness accounts*. The Gospel accounts are not written as mythical accounts – 'In a hole in the ground there lived a hobbit.' They are written as historical accounts which were dependent on witnesses and must be judged as such. If you want to investigate this further, then return to the book I recommended earlier, Bauckham's, *Jesus and the Eyewitnesses.*[3] It is not a light read, but it is well worth sticking with, providing you with the scholarly and historical evidence.

---

3.   Richard Bauckham, *Jesus and the Eyewitnesses: The Gospels as Eyewitness Testimony* (Grand Rapids, Michigan and Cambridge, U.K.: Eerdmans, 2006).

It has often been pointed out that it is of great significance that it was women who were the primary first witnesses. The witness of a woman was considered to be so untrustworthy that, to be equal to that of a man, there had to be another woman. If the disciples had made up the story of Jesus rising from the dead, the last thing they would have done is have women as the primary witnesses. Incidentally, that is not just true of first-century Jewish culture; it is also an attitude that exists today. Last Easter, I received a tweet from an atheist of impeccable liberal credentials attacking me for believing the witness of a few hysterical female prostitutes! Misogyny is alive and well in the modern world.

In this respect, as a historian I regard the different details recorded in the Gospels as further proof. This may sound somewhat strange to you. When you read through the four Gospel accounts, they read as different versions. Some people have seen this as weakening the evidence. Surely all the stories would have been the same if they were true? Not at all. We like to think that we remember everything in the past as it happens. The truth is that we have very selective memories and often filter out things, not because we are lying, but because we have limited mental capacity. In legal terms, there is a doctrine known as the Moorov doctrine. Let us suppose that you are accused of assaulting someone and they come forward with a complaint to that effect. Other than the testimony of the complainant, there is no evidence. On that basis, you cannot be convicted. However, suppose that three other people come forward with the same complaint; then there is the basis for a prosecution. But what ruins the case for the prosecution is four complainants all with exactly the same story identical in every detail. This would indicate that the four had got together and very likely colluded. Collusion is far less likely if there are four different stories, with different details, but the same substance and without contradiction. John Wenham's, *Easter Enigma*,[4] deals with this in a thoughtful and considered manner and I would recommend it for your further reading.

I can't go into all the resurrection appearances but my favourite is recorded in Luke 24, when Jesus appeared to the two disciples on the road to Emmaus. I love it because the details are so human and because, as is so often the case, the disciples really don't come across in an particularly flattering light. Any book which portrays its heroes in such an unflattering light is more likely to be true than one in which the good guys are always perfect.

The empty tomb

How is this to be explained? Apart from the swoon theory, there are a couple of others. First is what we call the conspiracy theory. The disciples stole the body. The first version of this is recorded by Matthew, who tells us that the

---

4.   Exeter: Paternoster Press, 1984.

chief priests and the elders bribed the Roman soldiers with 'a large sum of money' to lie and say that they had fallen asleep, and whilst they were asleep the disciples sneaked in and stole the body. It's not really very difficult to pick holes in this. For a start, Roman soldiers did not sleep on duty; to do so could result in extremely severe punishment, usually death. In that case, why did the soldiers agree to go along with the chief priests' plan? Because, as Matthew tells us, they were assured that the chief priests would ensure they were all right with the governor. However, even though the conspiracy theory does not make much sense, never forget that arguing with a conspiracy theorist is almost like being raised from the dead! Everything you say tends to be seen as part of the conspiracy.

The second theory is what we call the 'cock-up' theory. The women and the disciples went to the wrong tomb. They found it empty and then just made up a story about Jesus being seen alive. The trouble is that, in order to disprove this, all the authorities had to do was go to the right tomb and display the body. It was, after all, very prominent, sealed with a great stone and guarded by soldiers. In addition, the problem with both this theory and the conspiracy one is that it presupposes a level of planning and psychological strength in the disciples that was highly unlikely. They were discouraged, despondent and defeated. They were in a mood to go home and forget the last three years as a sorry mistake, and certainly in no state to make up stories that would eventually result in their deaths.

The resurrection appearances

These are carefully listed. Jesus appeared to the disciples by the Lake of Galilee, to more than five hundred at one time; to James, at a meal before Pentecost; and when He went back to heaven in what is known as the Ascension. The appearances were varied in place and time, physical, undramatic and unprecedented. It was the same Jesus, but different. These were not collective hallucinations, or mass hysteria. That would be psychologically very difficult to explain and still offers no explanation for the empty tomb. These were not ghost appearances. I love the details for example in Luke 24:42-43: 'They gave him a piece of broiled fish, and he took it and ate it in their presence.' Ghosts don't eat broiled fish. It was far more than a symbol.

N. T. Wright argues that either the empty tomb or the resurrection appearances would be sufficient on their own to justify the early Christian belief that Jesus had risen from the dead, but both combined provides powerful evidence.

> The claims can be stated once more in terms of necessary and sufficient conditions. The actual bodily resurrection of Jesus (not a mere resuscitation, but a transforming revivification) clearly provides a *sufficient* condition of the tomb being empty and the 'meetings' taking place.

Nobody is likely to doubt that. Once grant that Jesus really was raised and all the pieces of the historical jigsaw puzzle of early Christianity fall into place. My claim is stronger: that the bodily resurrection of Jesus provides a *necessary* condition for these things; in other words, that no other explanation could or would do. All the efforts to find alternative explanations fail, and they were bound to.[5]

I have read nothing better than N. T. Wright's tour de force on this subject, which is well worth reading if you really want to examine this evidence in greater detail.

Another key question for me is: were the apostles liars? Follow it through. Does it make sense? The human heart is fickle, changes and is open to bribery. Only one of them would have to have admitted the deception under threat of imprisonment, torture and death, and all would have been lost. But they didn't. The starting point for the apostles is the resurrection. They were prepared to, and did, die for that belief – not because they were fanatics or deluded, but because it was true, and being true, changed everything, including their own deaths. If Christ had not risen from the dead, and they knew it, then the whole game is completely changed.

And if Christ has not been raised, your faith is futile; you are still in your sins. Then those also who have fallen asleep

---

5.   N. T Wright, *The Resurrection of the Son of God* (London: SPCK, 2003), p. 717.

> in Christ are lost. If only for this life we have hope in Christ,
> we are to be pitied more than all men. (1 Cor. 15:17-19)

One factor often overlooked is the whole significance of the Sabbath. The Jewish day of rest was sacrosanct. It was an essential part of the disciples' culture and belief, but they changed from the Sabbath to what they called the Lord's Day? Why? Because it was the day that Christ was raised.

I would also add to these factors the *continued existence of the church*. The best explanation for the church not only existing, but also thriving and eventually outgrowing and outlasting the mighty Roman Empire, is the presence of the risen Christ. Think of the testimony of Saul (later to be better known as the apostle Paul). It was his encounter with the risen Christ that led to his conversion, the subsequent ministry planting many churches throughout the Roman Empire, and writing most of the New Testament letters. I love Augustine's take on this.

> And now we have three incredibles, all of which have yet come to pass. It is incredible that Jesus Christ should have risen in the flesh and ascended with flesh into heaven; it is incredible that the world should have believed so incredible a thing; it is incredible that a very few men, of mean birth and the lowest rank, and no education, should have been able so effectually to persuade the world, and even its learned men, of so incredible a thing.[6]

---

6.   St. Augustine, *City of God and Christian Doctrine*, p. 482.

He goes on to argue that the miracles of the apostles were the testimony to the resurrection of Christ, but that even the sceptics who do not accept these miracles are faced with the one great miracle, 'that the whole world has believed without any miracles'. Wishful thinking does not explain the church.

So what?

Do you know why most Protestants don't have crucifixes (crosses with Christ on them)? It is because the cross is empty – Christ has risen. Grant for a moment the possibility or truth of the resurrection. Tim Keller, at the Gospel Coalition conference in 2013, made an intriguing statement: 'Resurrection makes Christianity the most irritating religion on earth.' Why is that? Because you can argue about ethics, doctrines, rituals until you are blue in the face; people are free to believe what they want. What does it matter? But the resurrection means everything is changed. If Christ is not raised, then Christians are to be pitied for wasting our lives. But if Christ is raised, then that means it would be insane to ignore Him and His claims.

Rob Bell is another writer who just does not seem to grasp the wonder of the resurrection: 'So when the writers of the Bible talk about Jesus' resurrection bringing new life to the world, they aren't talking about a new concept. They're talking about something that has always been true. It's how the world works.' No, it is not how the world works. I'll tell you how the world works. Stand on a hillside at the grave of a young man in the Scottish Highlands. The scenery is dramatic; the weather is bleak, cold and windswept. You have just buried that young man. The way the world works is, that is it. His body is in the grave and will rot. The Christian has a different hope. I was standing at my father-in-law's grave on the island of Lewis with other mourners when I heard the minister say, in casual conversation: 'There is going to be some party here on the day of the resurrection!' I was astonished to hear a very traditional minister describe the resurrection in such terms; but he was right.

In the words of the singer/songwriter Garth Hewitt:

May you live to dance on your own grave,
May you live to boogie all night long.

At another time, I took the heartbroken parents of a 27-year-old friend, who had died suddenly, to the mortuary to identify his body. It was both distressing and incredible. His body was there, but he was not there. In the materialist world view, that is it. The end. Finito. But everything in our soul screams out – that is not right. 'He has made everything beautiful in its time. He has also set eternity in the hearts of men; yet they cannot fathom what God has done from beginning to end.'[7] We know there is something more. In my attempts to

---

7.   Ecclesiastes 3:11.

become an atheist I tried to conceive not existing but it was impossible. Why? Because as a human being I am made in the image of God and God has set eternity in my heart. The inner witness tells me death is not the end. The resurrection tells me death can be the door to a glorious new life.

The resurrection gives us a future and hope. It is personal, certain and unimaginably wonderful. Marvellous. We often sing a song in church, 'I stand amazed in the presence of Jesus the Nazarene ... how marvellous.' That is why Calvin declared, 'Let us, however, consider this settled; that no one has made progress in the school of Christ who does not joyfully await the day of death and final resurrection.'[8] He also urged us to reflect continually upon the resurrection: 'Accordingly, he alone has fully profited in the gospel who has accustomed himself to continual meditation upon the blessed resurrection.'[9]

But I accept that you are not yet in that place. You are still investigating. Perhaps it would be good for you to begin here.

The resurrection, therefore, is the place to begin if you are looking for a satisfying faith on which to base your life. Do not waste a lot of time investigating every religion under the sun from animism to Hinduism. Examine the evidence for the resurrection of Jesus instead. If he is risen you need look no further.[10]

---

8.   John Calvin, *Institutes of the Christian Religion*, 3:10:5.

9.   Ibid, 3:25:1.

10.   Michael Green, *The Day Death Died* (Leicester: InterVarsity Press, 1982), p. 60.

Meanwhile can I suggest that you have a look at John Betjeman's 1956 radio poem 'Three Crosses' which expresses that the wonderful hope that the resurrection brings?[11] A hope beautifully expressed in the Townend and Getty hymn 'See, What a Morning'. I leave you with the last verse.

> And we are raised with Him,
> Death is dead, love has won, Christ has conquered;
> And we shall reign with Him,
> For He lives: Christ is risen from the dead.[12]

Yours,

David

> Jesus said to her, 'I am the resurrection and the life. He who believes in me will live, even though he dies; and whoever lives and believes in me will never die. Do you believe this?' (John 11:25-26)

---

11. *Poems in the Porch: The Radio Poems of John Betjeman* (London: Bloomsbury, 2008), p. 115.

12. 'See, What a Morning' (Resurrection hymn). Words and Music by Keith Getty and Sutart Townend. Copyright © 2003 Kingsway Thankyou Music.

6 / MEANING

If people do not believe the word of Scripture, then they will not believe someone coming from the next world either. The highest truths cannot be forced into the type of empirical evidence that only applies to material reality.

Pope Benedict XVI[1]

Once you see that God is eternal, you will never again ask the question, 'who or what made God?' You will see that the question does not make sense.

Keith Ward[2]

Dear J,

You are absolutely right. I don't expect you to 'just believe' that Jesus rose from the dead. It is not something that can

1. Pope Benedict XVI, *Jesus of Nazareth: From the Baptism in the Jordan to the Transfiguration* (London: Bloomsbury Publishing, 2008), p. 216.

2. Keith Ward, *Why There Almost Certainly Is a God: Doubting Dawkins* (Oxford: Lion Books, 2008), p. 53.

easily be believed. That was as true in the first century as it is now. Hitchens and others portray first-century people as ignoramuses who thought resurrection was a regular and understandable occurrence. In fact, it was as ludicrous for them as it is for us. We are told, for example, that when Paul spoke to a group of Epicurean and Stoic philosophers at a meeting of the Areopagus in Athens he was doing fine until he spoke about the resurrection of the dead. At that point 'some of them sneered, but others said, "We want to hear you again on this subject"' (Acts 17:32). Plus ça change! I am glad that although you do not (yet!) accept the resurrection, you are willing to continue our correspondence and want to hear more.

Amongst the points you raise, can I deal with the one that I dealt with only in passing in my last letter? You ask about the possibility of the disciples' belief in resurrection being, in effect, a product of wishful thinking. Is it not the case that this is what they really wanted to happen and, given my earlier comments about how we remember the past selectively, perhaps all that happened was that they projected their wish that Christ should be alive and filtered out any inconvenient truths (like the fact that he was dead) from their memories and experience? In other words, they were self-deluded conspiracy theorists, who became so convinced of their delusion that they were prepared to die for it. While I grant that we can come up with examples of people who have believed something that was demonstrably false, and were even prepared to die for it, I cannot, however, put the disciples in that category. Why not? Because their belief in the resurrection was not demonstrably false. Forgive me. I didn't express that very well. Their belief in the resurrection could have been demonstrated to be false – it was all too easily falsifiable! All the authorities had to do was present the body of Jesus Christ. They could not and did not. Or, it could be a bit like the death of Hitler. We don't have Hitler's body because it was burned. I guess you could believe, if you wanted to, that he did not die, but escaped to Spain, and then eventually came to London, where for several years he ran a World War II memorabilia business. But you would, of course, have no evidence for this. You would have no witnesses describing his flight, no documents and no continuing business. It is not the same with Jesus. There were many witnesses and, rather than their testimony being nullified over the years, as more evidence came to light, it seems to have withstood the test of time.

Anyway, you were obviously in a particularly sharp frame of mind when you wrote to me. You remembered that in my first letter I had complained that Hitchens's *God is Not Great* was mistitled, because in that book he says virtually nothing about God. You point out that my response so far does not, at least directly, say a great deal about God. We have a man, Jesus Christ, born in unusual circumstances, doing unusual works, teaching some unusual things, dying an unusual death and ending up with an unusual post-death experience! But what does that have to say about God? A great deal. But I do have to warn you that, at this point, we are going to plunge into depths that may make your head hurt – being so beyond our limited world view.

In this respect, you will note the inconsistency in our atheist friends' understanding of the Jewish and Christian faiths. They like to portray the Bible as being written by a bunch of illiterate desert nomads (although quite how they manage to square the circle of illiterate people writing, I'm not sure!), whose limited knowledge and intellect were parochial. Hitchens, for example, writes: 'None of these provincials, or their deity, seems to have any idea of a world beyond the desert, the flocks and the herds, and the imperatives of nomadic substances.' The answer to that remarkably ignorant statement is just simply to read the first chapter of John's Gospel. It goes way beyond the desert into the vast reaches of eternity, the beginning of time and the nature and existence of God. And that is where we are going in this letter.

Unlike every other religion, Christianity makes a claim about its founder that is unique. We claim that Jesus *is* God, not that He simply points us to God or gives us the map to get there. Theoretically, every religion in the world does not need its founder. Except Christianity. 'If you take Christ out

of Christian, you just have ian. And Ian won't save you.'[3]
This is why we are talking about Christ. This is why saying
'Christianity is great' is not really addressing the heart of the
matter, because it gives the impression that Christianity, as
a system of doctrines, morals or rituals is great. But that is
not what we are saying – everything hangs on the fact that
Christ is great because Christ is both man and God.

Saul was a militant anti-Christian, even going so far as to
imprison followers of Christ and applaud the death of the
first Christian martyr, Stephen. Yet, after his own encounter
with the risen Jesus, and having changed his name to Paul,
he became the strongest advocate for a 'heresy', which was
so obnoxious to the Jews of his day that for many it meant
that anyone who believed it deserved the death penalty. Even
today, there are those who risk being imprisoned and killed
for teaching it (in stricter Muslim countries), or mocked and
ridiculed by our atheist friends. That heresy is, of course, the
doctrine of the Trinity. Paul, writing to the church in Rome,
declared that the significance of the resurrection was that it
proved that Christ was what He had claimed to be, the Son
of God. (Read Romans chapter 1, verses 1-4.) You have to
understand what a major paradigm shift in thinking that
was for a committed Jew. It's equivalent to Richard Dawkins
becoming a Catholic! Jesus was crucified for blasphemy, for

---

3.   Michael Ramsden, European Director of Ravi Zacharias International Ministries.

claiming to be the Son of God, thereby making Him equal to God. Furthermore, He claimed to do what only God could do, forgive sins, and He claimed that He had existed before Abraham: 'Before Abraham was, I am' (John 8:58). The essence of Judaism was that, in a world of polytheism, it was unapologetically monotheistic. The Shema – 'Hear O Israel, the Lord is our God, the Lord is one' – is the creed at the heart of Judaism. To Jews like Saul, it would have seemed as though the Christians were saying, 'the Lord is three'.

The Trinity

The revelation of God as Trinity is the cornerstone of Christian thinking. It is something that is prone to misunderstanding and misrepresentation. For example, a number of years ago we did a questionnaire in our local area. We asked people to rate, on a scale of one to five (with one being 'strongly agree with' and five being 'strongly disagree with') their opinion on various statements, one of which was 'Jesus is the Son of God'. What astonished us was the number of Muslims who, whilst they had either agreed or slightly disagreed with other biblical statements, strongly disagreed with this, and in some instances wrote some very strong remarks against the statement. I asked a friend who worked with Muslims why there was such a strong reaction on this particular question. 'You idiot,' he replied (he always had a subtle way with words!), 'you have just asked Muslims whether God had sex with the Virgin Mary and produced Jesus.' We were, of course, horrified. It is a classic example of how we need to be careful how we use words. We may think we are saying one thing, but people may be hearing another.

Long ago, the early-African Christian Augustine – who admittedly lived near the desert but could hardly by any measure be called ignorant or illiterate – recognized that we need to be really careful when talking about the Trinity. 'When the question is asked "what three?", human language labours altogether under great poverty of speech. The answer, however, is given, three "persons", not that it might be completely spoken, but that it might not be left wholly unspoken.'[4]

Whole forests have been felled to make enough paper to produce the number of books written on this subject, so I don't really expect to give you the knock-down, succinct proof – the explanation of the analogy of the Trinity. However, I would recommend a lovely little book by Professor Donald Macleod, entitled *Shared Life: The Trinity and the Fellowship of God's People*.[5] He explains the Bible's understanding of the Trinity in a simple and yet not simplistic way.

The Christian teaching of the Trinity is that there is indeed one God, who exists in three persons. The three

4.   St. Augustine, *On The Trinity*, Book V, Ch. 9.
5.   Donald Macleod, *Shared Life: The Trinity and the Fellowship of God's People* (Fearn, Ross-shire: Christian Focus Publications, 2000).

persons are distinct, yet are one in substance, essence or nature. The Father is God, the Son is God and the Spirit is God. The Father is not the Son or the Spirit. The Son is not the Father or the Spirit. The Spirit is not the Father or the Son. Three persons in one God. Try getting your head round that one! It is little wonder that the church speaks of the mystery of the Trinity. It is a mystery and yet it does make sense in so many ways.

Take, for example, the question of love. Hitchens boldly and courageously attacks this particular Christian doctrine: 'Compulsory love is another sickly element of Christianity.' He is certainly right in recognizing love as at the heart of Christianity. 'God is love. Whoever lives in love lives in God, and God in him' (1 John 4:16). But if love is of the essence of God, whom did God love before He created the world? The answer is that the Trinity shows God to be a fellowship of love, between Father, Son and Holy Spirit. There was a time when there was no world, nor people to love. But there was never a time when the Father was not loving the Son, and the Son loving the Father. Far from being a problem, the Trinity is the only truth about God which explains the existence of love. A totally solitary god might have many characteristics – power, wisdom, infinity of existence, etc. But until he creates someone to love, he cannot love. Therefore, for such a solitary god, love cannot be an essential characteristic of his nature.

It follows too that our salvation is trinitarian. The Father, Son and Spirit work in unison to bring about the salvation and redemption of mankind.

Not only so, but the church is trinitarian. Donald Macleod points out that just as the Trinity lives in equality, diversity and community, so the church must do the same. The triune God is love and we too must live in love.

Let me explain the importance of this in some words from another book in the New Testament, the book of Hebrews

> In the past God spoke to our forefathers through the prophets at many times and in various ways, but in these last days he has spoken to us by his Son, whom he appointed heir of all things, and through whom he made the universe. The Son is the radiance of God's glory and the exact representation of his being, sustaining all things by his powerful word. After he had provided purification for sins, he sat down at the right hand of the Majesty in heaven.[6]

What the writer is saying is that it is difficult for us to know God (Calvin once said that the two hardest things to know in the world are ourselves and God), but that God does reveal Himself to us. In the past, He spoke through the prophets in lots of different ways, but now He has given us the absolute and supreme revelation of Himself, and that is Jesus Christ.

---

6. Hebrews 1:1–3.

This is what the resurrection proves. If you want to know what God is like, look at Jesus, ask Jesus and listen to Jesus. Only the Son knows the Father. The only true knowledge of God comes through the Son. Now can you see why I regard Jesus as so important; why He is my 'magnificent obsession'?

The pre-existence of Christ

> In the beginning was the Word, and the Word was with God, and the Word was God. He was with God in the beginning. Through him all things were made; without him nothing was made that has been made. In him was life, and that life was the light of men. The light shines in the darkness, but the darkness has not understood it. (John 1:1-5)

If Jesus is God, then it means that He did not come into existence when He was born. And that is what the early church taught. Jesus was there before the beginning of the beginning. He was not created; He is the Creator. The term 'Word' here (*Logos* in Greek) is obviously referring to Him. Without Him nothing was made that has been made. At this point we need to pause and deal with an objection that you have raised before, and which is used as the ultimate argument by most atheists – who created the Creator? 'Thus the postulate of a designer or creator only raises the unanswerable question of who designed the designer or created the creator. Religion and theology and theodicy have consistently failed to overcome this objection'[7] I'm afraid that Hitchens has been outwitted in this one by that simple 'illiterate' fisherman, John. His answer to who created the Creator is – no one. There are things that have been made. Who made them? If the answer is everything that exists or can exist must have had a cause, and that cause had a cause, then that cause had a cause, what do you end up with? Causes all the way down; never-ending causes. You have to state that matter is eternal; that there was no beginning to the material universe. That does take an incredible amount of faith to believe, and indeed sets itself in opposition to the now universally accepted fact that the universe had a beginning – with the Big Bang about thirteen billion years ago. This would require not just faith, but blind faith (going against the evidence) on behalf of the atheist – the very thing I am often accused of by Mr Dawkins! When asked by the Edge Foundation, 'What do you believe is true even though you cannot prove it?' Dawkins replied: 'I believe that all life, all intelligence, all creativity and all "design" anywhere in the universe, is the direct or indirect product of Darwinian natural selection.'[8] Dawkins's rejection of the ultimate intelligence, the absolute being of God is a matter of belief without proof. It is a belief based on blind faith

---

7. *God Is Not Great*, p. 71.

8. Cited in Antony Flew, *There is a God* (New York: HarperCollins, 2008), p. xix.

and, like so many such beliefs, does not tolerate any kind of dissension or defection – but you are more open-minded. There is an alternative to that faith.

But what if the Bible is true? What if there is a Creator who is Himself uncreated? That is what the Bible teaches, and that is what we are told about Jesus. As the pre-existent Son, He has no beginning. There was a beginning – but He was not begun in the beginning. He was there. He was, He is, and He will be.

Let me give you another mind-blowing passage from one of those ignoramuses who had no idea of a world beyond the desert. Paul wrote about Jesus:

> He is the image of the invisible God, the firstborn over all creation. For by him all things were created: things in heaven and on earth, visible and invisible, whether thrones or powers or rulers or authorities; all things were created by him and for him. He is before all things, and in him all things hold together. (Col. 1:15-17)

I was at a stunning lecture in which the professor spoke about how 4 per cent of the universe was matter, about 25 per cent anti-matter, and the rest something that he called 'dark matter' – the substance that holds the universe together. We know that there is something that holds everything together. Paul claims that ultimately it is Christ. When he spoke to the Greeks in Athens he quoted the pagan poet, Epimenides, 'in him we live and move and have our being', and ascribed this ground of being to God (Acts 17:28).

So you can see where we are going with this. That Jesus is God is the central claim of Christianity. There really is no way round that. If Jesus was not the Son of God (in the trinitarian sense that I have outlined above) then he was a false, lying, wicked impostor, whose words are vain and meaningless, and who only intended to deceive. You just cannot get away with the 'I like Jesus, he was a good man, but he was not who he claimed to be' routine.

Despite all the best efforts of Dan Brown, there is no evidence that the early church had any doubts about the divinity of Jesus. If the Shema was the fundamental creed of Judaism, 'Jesus is Lord' was the fundamental creed of Christianity. Right from the beginning of the church, Jesus was worshipped as God. The Roman governor Pliny wrote in the second century of those who 'sang hymns to Christ as God'. The earliest Christian writings outwith the New Testament reflect that as well.

> For our God, Jesus Christ, now that He is with the Father, is all the more revealed in His glory. Christianity is not a thing of silence only but of manifold greatness (Epistle of Ignatius to the Romans).[9]

9. Alexander Roberts, et al (Eds), *The Ante-Nicene Fathers: the Writings of the Fathers Down to A.D. 325, Volume I: The Apostolic Fathers With Justin Martyr and Irenaeus* (New York: Cosimo, Inc., 2007), p.75.

> For Christ is King, and Priest, and God, and Lord, and angel, and man, and captain, and stone, and a Son born, and first made subject to suffering, then returning to heaven, and again coming with glory, and He is preached as having the everlasting kingdom: so I prove from all the Scriptures (Justin – *Dialogue with Trypho*).[10]

He emptied Himself

But I am getting a bit carried away – put it down to my Magnificent Obsession! If the resurrection proves that Jesus is the Son of God, and if that firms and clarifies the understanding of God as Trinity, lots of questions remain. What was Jesus doing before He was born? Why is there no indication of this Trinity in the Old Testament? Well, as Augustine again pointed out, the teaching of the New Testament is latent, not patent, in the Old Testament. There are hints and indications of this. The use of the term Elohim (which is plural) for God, for example, the use of the word 'us' in 'Let us make man in our image' (Gen. 1:26), the 'us' again referring to God in the plural. And there are at various times what are called, theophanies (appearances of God), in the historical narrative of the Old Testament – here the 'angel of the Lord' is sometimes seen as a pre-incarnation appearance of Christ.

Now we are getting to what the Trinity really means in speaking of the 'incarnation'. The resurrection proves to

---

10.   Ibid, p. 211.

us the identity of Christ as the Son of God, which in turn explains His miraculous birth. Christ being born really is 'Immanuel' – God with us. He is God incarnate.

> Your attitude should be the same as that of Christ Jesus:
> Who, being in very nature God,
>> did not consider equality with God something to be grasped,
> but made himself nothing,
>> taking the very nature of a servant,
>> being made in human likeness.
> And being found in appearance as a man,
>> he humbled himself
>> and became obedient to death—
>>> even death on a cross! (Phil. 2:5-8)

And so we have come full circle. The glorious second person of the Trinity was sent by the Father and enabled by the Spirit to live as a human being, show us the love of God through His teachings and miracles, die in our place so that our sins could be forgiven and be raised from the dead, before ascending into heaven. Marcus Brigstocke writes of his desire for God:

> I wish there was a God. I wish for that God to exist now and for all time. I wish to be fully conscious of God and more importantly for Him to be fully conscious of me. I wish for God to be powerful, infinitely wise, kind, loving, fair and, when necessary, willing to carry out humiliating and painful corrections on my fellow human beings.[11]

---

11. Marcus Brigstocke, *God Collar* (London: Transworld Publishers, 2012), p. 52.

Jesus is that eternal, conscious, powerful, wise, kind, loving, fair and just God.

In some senses the presence of Jesus on earth is a bit like the TV programme, *The Secret Millionaire*, in which a very wealthy person goes to live and work amongst the poor and only when the person has gone (and send on the subsequent cheque) do they realize just who they had amongst them. Jesus came and lived with us. We didn't recognize Him. We didn't know who He was. We mocked Him and we crucified Him. He was 'despised and rejected of men'. He made himself nothing, that we might become something. As Athanasius of Alexandria stated, 'He became what we are, that we might become what he is.'

Calvin, as always, puts it clearly:

> For the same reason it was also imperative that he who was to become our Redeemer be true God and true man. It was his task to swallow up death. Who but the Life could do this? It was his task to conquer sin. Who but very Righteousness could do this? It was his task to rout the powers of world and air. Who but a power higher than world and air could do this? Now where does life or righteousness, or lordship and authority of heaven lie but with God alone? Therefore our most merciful God, when he willed that we be redeemed, made himself our Redeemer in the person of his only-begotten Son. (Rom. 5:8)[12]

---

12. John Calvin, *Institutes of the Christian Religion*, 2:12:2.

And I love the way a much earlier Christian described the incarnation: 'He that hung up the earth in space was Himself hanged up; he that fixed the heavens was fixed with nails; He that bore up the earth was borne up on a tree; the Lord of all was subjected to ignominy in a naked body – God put to death! The King of Israel slain with Israel's right hand!' (Melito of Sardis, A.D. 160-177).[13]

One final question: if Jesus was raised from the dead, where is He now? Read Acts, chapter one, for the account of His being raised to heaven after forty days. Did Jesus remain human? Yes – as the nineteenth-century Scottish theologian, John 'Rabbi' Duncan put it, 'The dust of the earth is on the throne of the majesty on high.' Why did He not stay? Would it not have been easier for people to believe if He were still around on earth? No, because He had a human body and therefore was limited. So instead He sent His Holy Spirit on the day of Pentecost. It is the Spirit who now takes all these glorious truths about Jesus and applies them to people. 'The Holy Spirit is the bond by which Christ effectually unites us to himself'.[14] There it is again – the Trinity working together in love for our good!

I hope you can see that Christopher Hitchens's attack on religion in general, and Christianity in particular, does

13. Alexander Roberts, et al (Eds), *The Ante-Nicene Fathers: the Writings of the Fathers Down to A.D. 325, Volume 8* (Grand Rapids, Michigan: Eerdmans., 1986), p. 757.

14. John Calvin, *Institutes of the Christian Religion*, 3:1:1.

not even remotely begin to address the rich teaching and meaning given through the Bible about the person and work of Jesus Christ, and the incredible greatness of God. He *is* great, because of who He is and what He has done. I leave you with one of the trinitarian blessings of the early church: 'May the grace of the Lord Jesus Christ, and the love of God, and the fellowship of the Holy Spirit be with you all' (2 Cor. 13:14).

Yours in Christ,

David

> In the beginning was the Word, and the Word was with God, and the Word was God. He was with God in the beginning. Through him all things were made; without him nothing was made that has been made. In him was life, and that life was the light of men. The light shines in the darkness, but the darkness has not understood it. (John 1:1-5)

7 / MISSION

These that have turned the world upside down are come hither also.

Acts 17:6, KJV

Christopher Hitchens's book [*God Is Not Great*] was an absolute shambles – he knows absolutely nothing about the history of religion, and I mean *nothing*.

Camille Pagila[1]

Dear J,

Thank you for being so patient with me. I realize that my last letter contained a lot that is way out of your comfort zone – and to be honest it is way out of mine as well. But surely that is the point. We are not going to restrict reality to the world that only we can understand or recognize. In

---

1.   Interview in *Third Way*, Vol. 31, No. 9, Nov. 2008, p. 21.

the words of Mulder and Scully from *The X-Files*, 'The Truth is out there'! We have to find it or it has to find us. This, of course, is the great contention of Jesus Christ, that He is the Truth who has found us. Truth is embodied in a person who is also the Way and the Life.

You were a bit puzzled about my explanation as to why Jesus ascended into heaven, and why it was better for Him to go. I accept my explanation was somewhat inadequate, but perhaps it is better to explain it in terms of the story of one of the early converts to Christianity: Lydia, a businesswoman from the city of Philippi in Macedonia. One Saturday she went down to the river, as was her habit, to worship God. The apostle Paul came along and gave his message about the risen Christ. She responded by becoming a believer and she, and her whole household, were then baptized, and thus began the church in Philippi. Why did she believe? Because 'the Lord opened her heart to respond to Paul's message' (Acts 16:14). That is how Christianity works. It is not imposed by force, whether of words or weapons. The message of God loving the world so much that He sent His Son is preached by the church, and applied by the Spirit to the heart ('heart' in biblical terms refers not just to love, but to the whole centre of the human personality). It is always the triune God working for the good of His people.

Our road so far has led us from the birth of Christ, forward to His death and resurrection, and then back into the counsels of eternity, to a time before time began. But we are not finished yet. In fact, all of this would have been useless to us unless we heard about it. Good news is not good news to those who do not hear. If, as looked highly likely, the early church had been strangled at birth, then the past two thousand years of history would not have happened, and we would not be discussing Jesus Christ today. The survival and growth of the Christian church over the past two millennia is itself miraculous, and is a crucial part of the evidence that Bertrand Russell demanded. When Christ said, 'I will build my church and the gates of Hades will not prevail against it,' He meant it. And He has been proved true.

When you think about the history of the church, I wonder what goes through your head: the Crusades, burning of witches, the Inquisition? The cultural supremacy of the atheistic mindset in the twentieth century has resulted in a rewriting of history so that, at least in much of the popular mindset, the narrative is one in which the church is associated with this host of negatives. It is a caricature, but like all caricatures there is an element of truth within it. Therefore, even Christians have fallen into the trap of accepting the caricature and distancing ourselves from the history of the church. Doubtless you have heard the line, 'I like Jesus Christ, but I don't like the church.' This is often said by people who know neither Jesus Christ nor the church, but are just judging on the basis of impression and feeling. Yet that cultural zeitgeist is now so deeply ingrained that, everywhere I go to speak, I am accosted by people who accuse me of being an apologist for everything from slavery to Adolf Hitler (he was a Catholic, don't you know?)!

I cannot possibly deal exhaustively with all the issues raised, but I would encourage you to read the history of the church (from a variety of different perspectives). As a historian, I love reading and thinking about history, and would strongly recommend that you actually do read books and primary sources, if possible, rather than simply rely on Google and Wikipedia. Every week, I am presented with 'facts' and 'quotes' by people who have not read the subjects concerned, but instead have just indulged in the rather easy and lazy practice of quote-mining. I am astonished, for example, at how many atheists must have read *Mein Kampf*, given the number of times they use the quote about Hitler calling Jesus his Lord. The trouble is that, for the vast majority, this quotation is all they have read (usually from another atheist blog or website). They have not read the book, they don't know the context and history of the period, and they know precious little about the life and thought of Adolf Hitler. This quote is enough for them (combined with the fact that he was baptized as a Roman Catholic). It is important to remember that a statement without a context just becomes a pretext for whatever particular prejudice we want to put forward. Christians can be as guilty of this as anyone else – I have read some incredible statements from Christians that are made without any other supporting evidence, other than 'I read it somewhere.' The deathbed conversion of Charles Darwin is one such 'urban myth'.

The early church

The second part of Dr Luke's two-part account of the early church (his first being the Gospel of Luke) is known as the Acts of the Apostles. His introduction to that is fascinating: 'In my former book, Theophilus, I wrote about all that Jesus began to do and to teach until the day he was taken up to heaven, after giving instructions through the Holy Spirit to the apostles he had chosen' (Acts 1:1-2). You will note that he speaks of what Jesus *began* to do and to teach – the implication being that His teaching and doing *continued* after He ascended into heaven. The book of Acts records how the early church was birthed, developed and grew, spreading from Jerusalem on the day of Pentecost, to its ending with Paul's house arrest in Rome. It is a fascinating story of courage, persecution, miracles, new churches and incredible growth. From the very beginning, the Christian church has always been a missionary church.

> Being with Jesus and being sent by him seem at first sight
> mutually exclusive, but they clearly belong together. The
> Apostles have to learn to be with him in a way that enables
> them, even when they go to the ends of the earth, to be with

him still. Being with him includes the missionary dynamic by its very nature, since Jesus' whole being is mission.[2]

The Epistle to Diognetus, written less than a hundred years after the death of Christ, indicates one of the reasons why Christians had such an impact in the Roman Empire.

The Christians are distinguished from other men, neither by country, nor language, nor the customs they observe. The course of conduct which they follow has not been devised by any speculation or deliberation of inquisitive men; nor do they, like some, proclaim themselves the advocates of any merely human doctrines. But, inhabiting Greek as well as Barbarian cities, according as the lot of each of them has determined, and following the customs of the nations in respect to clothing, food, and the rest of their ordinary conduct, they display to us their wonderful and confessedly striking method of life. ... They marry as do all; they beget children, but they do not destroy their offspring. They have a common table but not a common bed. They are in the flesh, but they do not live after the flesh. They pass their days on earth, but they are citizens of heaven.[3]

2. Pope Benedict XVI, *Jesus of Nazareth: From the Baptism in the Jordan to the Transfiguration* (London: Bloomsbury Publishing, 2008), p. 172.

3. Alexander Roberts, et al (Eds), *The Ante-Nicene Fathers: the Writings of the Fathers Down to A.D. 325, Volume I: The Apostolic Fathers With Justin Martyr and Irenaeus* (New York: Cosimo, Inc., 2007), p. 26.

A pagan writer, Lucian of Samosata, in A.D. 170 gave his reasons for the growth of Christianity:

> The Christians you know, worship a man to this day—the distinguished personage who introduced their novel rites, and was crucified on that account. …You see, these misguided creatures start with the general conviction that they are immortal for all time, which explains their contempt of death and their voluntary self-devotion which are so common among them; and then it was impressed on them by their original lawgiver that they are all brothers, from the moment they are converted, and deny the gods of Greece, and worship the crucified sage, and live after his laws.[4]

Apart from the fact that Christians were prepared to die for their faith (note that they were not prepared to kill for their faith), this testimony reminds me of the words of Christ, 'All men will know you are my disciples if you have love one for another' (John 13:35).

By the way, did you know that the early Christians were called atheists by the surrounding Greco-Roman culture? Why? Because they did not have temples, sacrifices and a priestly caste. 'And we confess that we are atheists, as far as gods of this sort are concerned, but not with respect to the most true God, the Father of righteousness and temperance

---

4.   Lucian, *The Death of Peregrine*, in *The Works of Lucian of Samosata*, trans. by H.W. Fowler and F. G. Fowler, 4 vols. (Oxford: Clarendon Press, 1949), vol. 4.

and the other virtues, who is free from all impurity.'[5] This was written in the early second century. Yet, when our modern atheists make the point that Christians are atheists to all the other gods, and they as atheists just go one god further – they think they are making a stunning original point, which no-one had thought of until they came along! The fact is that, right from the beginning, the Christians knew they were giving up on all the so-called gods, and that Jesus was not just another god. He is the second person of the Trinity, the only Creator and almighty God.

What is the church?

Augustine said that he who does not have the church for his mother cannot have God for his Father. Which leads us to ask – what is the church? It is the *ecclesia,* the called-out assembly of the people of God. You will note that I speak of the church – which creates a problem when we consider the many hundreds of denominations and different churches. Am I saying that my small denomination is the only true one? Not at all. There are different understandings of just exactly how a church should be governed, as well as different understandings of secondary teachings in terms of theology and doctrine. But I would argue that the church of Jesus Christ is one through all the ages, and is – as Christ

---

5.   *The First Apology of Justin Martyr*, in Alexander Roberts, et al (Eds), *The Ante-Nicene Fathers: Volume I*, p. 164.

Himself taught – His bride. I realize that it can get very confusing, with all the different denominations, and claims and counter-claims. Personally, I don't really have that much difficulty with the existence of different traditions. God has preserved and kept His church in many different forms, and will continue to do so. In fact it could be argued that the very flexibility of the church, and its ability to adapt to different cultures, is one of the reasons it has continued to grow.

The key element, though, has to be that the church is the *church of Jesus Christ*. He founds it; He is the rock on which it is built, and when she moves away from Christ she stops being the church. 'I am only saying that the blessed and happy state of the Church always had its foundation in the person of Christ.'[6]

There is a simple point here. Christ is the foundation of the church, not nationality, class, priests, kings or queens. He is the foundation and the head. How much trouble would have been avoided if those who call themselves Christians and churches had remembered and practised this. 'In the church are mingled many hypocrites who have nothing of Christ but the name and outward appearance.'[7] Our atheist friends are very clever here. They mix and match

---

6. John Calvin, *Institutes of the Christian Religion*, 2:6:2.

7. Ibid, 4:1:7.

two doctrines. Firstly, they agree with Jesus' teaching about hypocrisy being one of the worst sins, and gleefully point out the hypocrisies of many who claim the name of Christ; then, secondly, they put their own hypocritical doctrine of equality into the equation (hypocritical because they exclude themselves from this equation). They declare that it would not be right to condemn one particular person or group – so let's condemn them all! If one Christian does something wrong, then all Christians are to be blamed. If one church gets something wrong then all are tainted. Guilt by association. This is a shallow and superficial view. It does not take into account the Bible's teaching that all people, including Christians, are sinners and therefore, of course, Christians are going to do things that are wrong. Nor does this view take in the obvious observation that not every group that professes to be a church is a church. If we point this out, they protest, 'But who are you to judge?' And thus, in the name of being non-judgmental, they judge us all. The great Catholic apologist G. K. Chesterton once said, 'The Church is justified, not because her children do not sin, but because they do.' Indeed, as I said in a previous letter, one of the reasons I believe is that the doctrine of total depravity (as we call it) rings true here as much as anywhere else!

You might ask but how then can we know what a real church is?

'Whenever we see the Word of God purely preached and heard, and the sacraments administered according to Christ's institution, there, it is not to be doubted, a church of God exists.'[8] Christ alone is head of the church. He alone should reign and rule over it. His authority is exercised and administered by His Word. Augustine again writes (I trust Mr Hitchens would forgive me; I have a tendency to keep forgetting how ignorant Augustine is when he writes such sublime statements as this!): 'Our Lord Christ has bound the fellowship of the new people together with sacraments very few in number, very excellent in meaning, very easy to observe.'[9]

Of course, there are going to be hypocrites and false churches, but just because there is the false does not exclude the real. Counterfeit banknotes only exist because real ones do. Counterfeit Christianity only exists because there is real Christianity. Sadly, of course, throughout history, and still today, there have been those who shame the name of Jesus Christ, by living lives contrary to the faith they profess. This is even worse when it is church leaders who do so. But again, you cannot catch me out here, because this is just what Jesus prophesied: 'How often did Christ and his apostles foretell that pastors would pose the greatest dangers to the church?'[10]

---

8.   Ibid, 4:1:9.

9.   Cited in ibid, 4:10:14.

10.   Ibid, 4:9:4.

Sorry, I just realized I have been making a big assumption. I keep talking about the Word of God and Christ ruling the church through His Word, and I realize that that leaves a lot of questions. How do we know what the Bible actually is? Is it not the case that at the Council of Nicea, in A.D. 325, the church decided to keep some books and got rid of a whole lot of others which were considered to be inconvenient? No – that is another myth in the Dan Brown mould. The Bible that we have is the Old Testament as Jesus had it, and the New Testament. The New consists of twenty-seven books, four of which are Gospels, the book of Acts, the apocalyptic book of Revelation, and the rest are all letters, mostly to churches but some to individuals within the first-century church. Why were these twenty seven included and others which have come to light excluded? The criteria were quite simple. Only those books which were considered to be apostolic (either written by, or approved by the apostles) were recognized. The manuscript support for what is called the canon of the New Testament is very strong – we have over five thousand extant manuscripts from the first three centuries of the Christian church. For ancient historical documents this is extraordinary and without precedent. The story of the transmission and preservation of the Bible is an incredible tale in itself, and one well worthy of your investigation.

Did Christianity spread by violence?

Let's move past early church history, the Middle Ages and come on to the Reformation. You will have noticed I cite Calvin a lot. For Hitchens, he is a kind of bogeyman: 'a sadist, and torturer and killer, who burned Servetus'.[11] Except that Calvin did not burn Servetus, did not torture him and did not kill him. It was the Council of Geneva who ordered his execution by burning. Calvin thought he deserved the death penalty, but pled for a more humane execution and prayed with him beforehand. As I said, it is not the Christian way to kill people for either not converting or for being heretics. In the zeitgeist of the sixteenth century, Calvin was actually a reformer of society as well as the church. It's funny, I kind of bought into the Calvin-as-bogeyman theory, until I actually read his writings and some of the better biographies. I find him to be a humble and gracious man, who had personality flaws and faults, but who had a deep sense of dependence on God, consciousness of his own sin and who did more to reform and advance European society than almost any other person of that era. But the atheist zeitgeist is to hunt round for one thing that he did that in modern eyes was wrong, and condemn everything else on that basis. If we were all treated like that, I wonder if any of us would survive!

---

11. Christopher Hitchens, *God Is Not Great* (London: Atlantic Books, 2007), p. 233.

But let's ask about other forms of violence in 'Christian' countries. There is no doubt that once the apostle Paul was told to go west to Greece, rather than east to Asia, European and world history was changed. When the Emperor Constantine was converted to Christianity in A.D. 312, it marked the transformation of the church from being a persecuted and much maligned minority to eventually becoming the official religion of the Roman Empire. We can argue about how much that was a good or bad thing but, from that point on, for many European countries and for most of subsequent European history, church and state were intertwined. This means that we run into a problem when we consider the whole question of whether the church used violence. So, for example, were the Crusades primarily religious, political or economic? Did the church burn witches, or was it councils and governments? We also really need to find out the facts as well as the context of what is involved.

Many people seem to have the idea that the church burnt or drowned millions of witches and that the Inquisition was responsible for the death of hundreds of thousands more. But the nearest figures we have are that perhaps 40,000 women were killed as witches over a period of two hundred years – that is two hundred per year over the whole of Europe. It is, of course, two hundred per year too many, but hardly the holocaust that it is often portrayed as. As for the Inquisition, the last figures I saw suggested that there were 6,000 deaths over 500 years. That is horrendous, and I would not attempt to justify or excuse it in the name of Christ, but again it is not quite the story that we are led to believe. To generalize as Hitchens does – 'All religions take care to silence or to execute those who question them'[12] – is, to say the least, intellectually disingenuous.

The trouble is that once the church had political power, it became necessary for those in pursuit of political power to belong to the church. Then, of course, it becomes very difficult to distinguish between those who belong to the church because they follow Jesus, and those who belong to the church because they want power. We must admit there are those who do have a false theology (e.g., Jesus wants us to burn heretics) and in their religious zeal cause a great deal of harm. Zeal without knowledge and love is always dangerous, but perhaps especially so when it is linked with religion.

'The temptation to use power to secure the faith has risen again and again in varied forms throughout the centuries, and again faith has risked being suffocated in the embrace of power.'[13] Now you may find it interesting that I again quote the Pope. Has not the papacy done precisely that which Pope Benedict warns about? I agree. The mixture of political and religious power that has far too often been found in the

---

12.   Ibid, p. 125.

13.   Pope Benedict XVI, *Jesus of Nazareth*, 2008, p. 40.

papacy has done a great deal of harm. What I would urge you to do is recognize that this is not necessarily Christianity. You may be aware that there are some Christians who would argue that the Pope is the anti-Christ anyway, and therefore cannot be a Christian. To me, that is as simplistic and nonsensical as saying every Pope represents Christ. We do not live in such a black-and-white world. There are doubtless some Popes who have been followers of Jesus and others who have been lying hypocrites for whom the lowest place in hell is reserved! Please don't equate everything that is done in the name of Christ with Christ. But then I guess you can legitimately ask me, 'Is this not having it both ways?' When we see some of the good coming from Christianity, we claim it; when we see the bad, we disclaim it. Can I suggest that it is a little more nuanced than that? I accept fully that Christians and churches, including me and mine, will do things that are wrong and even evil. I accept that both because I observe it first hand, and because I believe what Jesus says about the pervasiveness of human sinfulness. However, I also accept that though we are still sinners, it is possible to know Christians by their fruits, and that any work of God in a human being will demonstrate something of the fruit of the Spirit, and any church of Christ will show something of the beauty of Christ – in the midst of all the sin and ugliness.

The Christian way is not about power but about the way of the cross – every generation needs to learn that.

What have the Christians ever done for us?

Do you remember the hilarious *Monty Python* sketch where John Cleese, acting as the leader of a Jewish liberation group, asks, 'What have the Romans ever done for us?' One of his followers mentions the aqueducts. The others go on to mention a long list of things which results in Cleese asking, 'What have the Romans ever done for us – apart from sanitation, the roads, irrigation, medicine, education, public health, wine, law and order, and peace!' What have Christians ever done for us? Yes, we can list the faults of those who profess to be Christians who have done great harm. But the good done in the name of Christ is quite astonishing.

> The gospel not only converts the individual, but it changes society. On every mission field from the days of William Carey, the missionaries carried a real social gospel. They established standards of hygiene and purity, promoted industry, elevated womanhood, restrained anti-social customs, abolished cannibalism, human sacrifice and cruelty, organised famine relief, checked tribal wars, and changed the social structure of society.[14]

Education (every major European university was founded on Christian principles), social reform, medicine, democracy, the arts and modern science all owe much of their current existence

---

14. Samuel Zwemer, Professor of Missions at Princeton, cited in Bill Bright: http://webparts.ccci.org/growth/transferable-concepts/07-how-you-can-help-fulfill-the-great-commission/02-who-of-great-commission.aspx.

to the teaching and ideas of the followers of Jesus Christ. That's a bold claim but one I think that can be substantiated. Take, for example, the question of science. As many have recognized, rather than being suppressed by the church, modern science stems from a theistic culture and indeed would have been impossible without the understanding that there was an ordered universe created by God. I find that faith in Christ and science go together, feeding off one another. 'Far from belief in God being some sort of irrational leap of faith it is the most rational hypothesis there is; and perhaps it is the only plausible and sure foundation of the rationality of the universe that science presupposes.'[15]

My own small nation of Scotland sent doctors, engineers, military men, politicians and missionaries all over the globe. For many, not all, the primary motivating factor was their Christian faith. We were one of the most literate and educationally advanced nations in the world, thanks largely to John Knox's maxim that where there was a church, there should be a school. It may just be a 'coincidence', but I don't think it is without significance that as Scotland has rapidly secularized so we have rapidly dumbed down, with one in five Scots now being functionally illiterate.

Sticking with this question of education, do you recall this remark from Hitchens? 'However the impressive fact

---

15. Keith Ward, *Why There Almost Certainly Is a God: Doubting Dawkins* (Oxford: Lion Books, 2008), p. 82.

remains that all religions have staunchly resisted any attempt to translate their sacred texts into languages "understood of the people" as the Cranmer prayer book phrases it.'[16] I read and reread that remark to try to make some sense of it. This is because it is one of the most easily refutable and self-contradictory remarks you could come across, and again just shows how even great intellects can be led into irrationality by prejudice. Because, of course, the essence of the English Reformation, as cited by Cranmer, was to translate the Bible into the common language of the people. It is bizarre to cite a religious leader advocating that their religious text should be translated, in order to claim that all religions resist attempts to translate their religions.

Speaking of education, I went to the University of Edinburgh, founded by Christianity, and funded by a welfare state established on Christian principles, to study history. One of my specialist subjects was the English Civil War and, as part of that, I had to read a book by the Marxist historian Christopher Hill, *The World Turned Upside Down*. I loved it and learned a great deal from it; although I disagreed with his presupposition that God had nothing to do with the tremendous social, political and economic changes at that time. In fact, the Bible verse which provided the title of that book (Acts 17:6) has become a kind of theme verse for

16.   Christopher Hitchens, *God Is Not Great*, p. 125.

my own ministry in and through the church. Tolstoy, in his agonizing about society and how to transform it, mused that everyone seemed to think about changing society; no one thought about changing their own hearts. The radicalness of Christianity is that it changes society by changing people.

I realize as I finish that this is so broad a sweep as to be almost impossible, but I am sure you get the drift. From the time of Jesus Christ, His church, with all its faults and imperfections, *has* fulfilled His mission. His work has continued and the world has been turned upside down.

Yours etc.,

David

> We always thank God, the Father of our Lord Jesus Christ, when we pray for you, because we have heard of your faith in Christ Jesus and of the love you have for all the saints— the faith and love that spring from the hope that is stored up for you in heaven and that you have already heard about in the word of truth, the gospel that has come to you. All over the world this gospel is bearing fruit and growing, just as it has been doing among you since the day you heard it and understood God's grace in all its truth. (Col. 1:3-6)

8 / MODERN

The urge to ban and censor books, silence dissenters, condemn outsiders, invade the private sphere, and invoke an exclusive salvation is the very essence of totalitarianism.

Christopher Hitchens, *God is Not Great*[1]

Lord, save me from your followers!

Bumper sticker seen on car in America

Dear J,

Again I thank you for your thoughtful and challenging response. In fact, much of what you have written anticipates what I wanted to write in this letter, so if you don't mind instead of attempting the impossible task of giving you a full picture of what Jesus is doing today through His church,

---

1.   Christopher Hitchens, *God Is Not Great* (London: Atlantic Books, 2007), p. 234.

I will spend most of the rest of this letter dealing with some of the issues that you raise.

Let's continue our journey. Here's another way of summarizing where we have got to so far. God, as the Creator of the world, made human beings in His own image, with knowledge, rationality, morality and personhood. Mankind, using our own freewill, fell from our original state and the world became distorted and polluted through that human rebellion against God (sin). God did not leave us to stew in our own sin and destroy ourselves. Instead He devised a plan to redeem us. This plan exploded into history in the person and work of His Son, Jesus Christ, who was miraculously born, taught us God's message, showed us God's power, and then died our death, and suffered our hell. He was raised from the dead and ascended into heaven, but on the Day of Pentecost, He sent His Holy Spirit who established His church and gave and preserved His Word. The combination of Jesus acting through the Spirit, the church, and the Word, has been enormously potent. With many ups and downs, the church has continued to grow, so that today we have ended up with about one third of the people in the world professing to be followers of Christ, and 20 per cent of the world being Muslims, who revere Jesus as a prophet. Not bad for a Palestinian peasant from two thousand years ago!

But what about today? Is this, as some people think, the end of the Christian era? Are we entering a new age of human enlightenment, or reverting to a Greco-Roman paganism or the many forms of New Age feel-good religion? Your questions are actually very helpful in answering this question so let's just stick with them.

Isn't there an inevitable progression from polytheism to monotheism to atheism?

I see you have been listening to our New Atheist friends. It is part of their creed (and I hinted at it in one of my letters), and one of their stock-in-trade, that 'Christians are atheists to all other gods except Jesus; atheists just go one god more.' The problem with this statement, as we have seen, is that it presupposes that Jesus is just one of the other man-made gods. He is not man-made, and therefore He cannot be unmade by men! However, that does not stop us trying.

Actually, the biggest danger to the Christian church does not come from persecution without, but from heresy within. This has always been the case throughout the church's history. Augustine warned: 'The heretics themselves also, since they are thought to have the Christian name and sacraments, Scriptures, and profession, cause great grief in the hearts of the pious, both because many who wish to be Christians are compelled by their dissensions to hesitate, and many evil-speakers also find in them matter for blaspheming the Christian name, because they too are at any rate *called* Christians' (emphasis mine).[2]

---

2. St Augustine, *City of God,* Book XVIII, ch. 51.

There are Christians who believe that the number-one reason for not believing is the problem of suffering, and atheists who believe that the number-one reason for not believing is that the certainties of science are supposed to conflict with the myths of faith. Personally I find a bigger reason to be the hypocrisies, false teaching and nonsense that sometimes go on in the church.

When U2 sang 'Bullet the Blue Sky' during the *Joshua Tree* album tour in the late 1980s, two lines in that song stood out, about TV evangelists:

Stealing money from the sick and the old
Well the God I believe in isn't short of cash, mister! [3]

The fact that people use religion to exploit other people is clear; the sadness for me is that the beautiful good news of Jesus is distorted and perverted in this way. Bono explained his revulsion as a believer to this kind of behaviour. 'I go to America and I turn on my television set, and I start sweating profusely because these guys have turned faith into an industry. It's appalling. It's ugly – the guy's hand is virtually coming out of the television set.'[4] I accept, of course, that Bono, who has made a fortune out of singing about social justice, is himself open to the charge of hypocrisy, and yet neither you nor I are

3.   These lines were not retained in the studio version.

4.   Bono speaking in 1987. in Steve Stockman, *Walk On: The Spiritual Journey of U2* (Relevant Books, 2001), p. 61.

in a position to judge, because we don't know what he has done with the money. That's another great advantage of being a Christian; we leave God to do the ultimate judging!

Of course, it is always wrong to tar everyone with the same brush. There are Christian preachers who use the medium of TV well and do so with honesty – but it does seem as though it is a medium that does not lend itself well to the Christian message, and is ripe for exploitation. Mind you, it's not only religious people who use religion to make money! A church in London asked me to debate Christopher Hitchens, something which I would have been delighted to do. He agreed, and it looked as though we would be able to go ahead with it, until we received the demands from his agent. Two first-class return tickets, London to New York, and $50,000. When the church pointed out that they were a church and did not have those kinds of resources, he agreed to cut the charge (because it was a charity) to $25,000. I think I said a return rail fare from Dundee and a bottle of malt would have done me! When the church said that that was still way beyond their means, the agent said that churches in the U.S.A. were prepared to pay that kind of money. More fool them. It is beyond irony that Richard Dawkins and his supporters are happy to accuse those who dare to write challenging his words of being 'fleas seeking to make a living off a dog's back', whilst he himself has greatly profited from rehashing old, tired arguments about the non-existence of God, and about how those who say they believe in God are either ignorant or just out to make money!

Wasn't Hitler a Christian?

If you are asking if Hitler was a follower of Jesus Christ, the answer is absolutely 'No'. If you mean, 'Was he baptized as a Roman Catholic, and did he sometimes make positive references to Christianity in his public speeches, and did he try to get the churches on his side?' then 'Yes'. But he was not a Christian in any meaningful sense of the word. He did not read the Bible, go to church, or follow Jesus. He hated God's chosen people, the Jews. It is difficult to see how someone who hated the Jews could follow the greatest Jew of all, Jesus Christ! As his ideologue, Martin Bormann, put it: 'National Socialism and Christianity are irreconcilable ... National Socialism is based on scientific foundations ... National Socialism on the other hand must always, if it is to fulfil its job in the future, be organized according to the latest knowledge of scientific research ... the concepts of Christianity ... in their essential points have been taken over from Jewry.'[5]

At this point, you can go and google lots of atheists who use the same quotes all the time to show that Hitler was a practising Christian. Even this week I was quoted this one by Hitler: 'Secular schools can never be tolerated because

---

5. Martin Bormann, in John S. Conway, *The Nazi Persecution of the Churches, 1933-1945* (Vancouver, B.C.:Regent College Publishing, 2001), p. 383.

such schools have no religious instruction.' That's it then. See? Hitler supported Christian schools because he wanted religious instruction; he must have been a Christian. But remember what we said about context? What was the context of that remark? That quote is from April 26, 1933, a speech made during negotiations leading to the Nazi-Vatican Concordat. It does not take a genius to work out why Hitler would speak in favour of Catholic schools (the vast majority of schools in Germany were either Catholic or Lutheran) in front of Catholics, when he was still in a position of trying to consolidate his power. Once you know the particular cultural and historical context of the quote, it changes it considerably.

Doesn't religion restrict freedom?

'The urge to ban and censor books, silence dissenters, condemn outsiders, invade the private sphere, and invoke an exclusive salvation is the very essence of totalitarianism' (Christopher Hitchens).[6] Religion does very often restrict freedom. But again we come back to tarring everyone with the same brush. It is clearly demonstrable that anti-religion can also restrict freedom. By definition, every healthy society must exercise some kind of restriction. Would you really want to live in a society where everything could be published? The minute you state that child pornography should not be published you have breached the principle of absolute

---

6.   Christopher Hitchens, *God Is Not Great,* p. 234.

freedom of speech. Every society is going to offer some kind of restriction; the only question is where you draw the line. Overall, I think you will find that societies which have been based upon biblical principles tend to offer a far greater freedom than those which have replaced God with the State. Have totalitarian states in the modern world been Christian? I am struggling to think of any that could seriously be called such. On the other hand, it's not difficult to think of atheistic or other religious states which fit the bill.

Whilst Hitler may not have been a card-carrying atheist (the jury is still out on that one), Stalin, Mao and Pol Pot definitely were. Stalin is particularly interesting. As a teenager, he came across *The Origin of Species* and, after staying up all night reading it, he found atheism. 'God's not unjust, he doesn't actually exist. We've been deceived. If God existed, he'd have made the world more just.'[7] When asked how he could be sure, he gave his friend a copy of Darwin. This lack of belief in God was not just a simple atheism, but also rather a bitter anti-theism. When he went to visit an old church with a friend who was the son of a priest, Stalin encouraged him to pull down an icon, smash it and urinate on it. 'Not afraid of God?' asked Stalin. 'Good for you!' Now, of course, the standard retort comes from our atheist friends: 'Stalin was an atheist – so what?

---

7.   Simon Sebag Montefiore, *Young Stalin* (Weidenfeld & Nicolson, 2007), p. 40.

He also had a moustache, but you don't blame everyone who has a moustache for Stalinism.' I hope you can see the facetiousness of that argument. If Stalin had attacked barbers, or sought to impose moustaches on everyone, then it would be relevant. The reason he destroyed churches, banned Christianity from public education, and sent thousands of Christians to their deaths was not because he had a moustache! Furthermore, they are missing the point somewhat. Stalin (and incidentally Hitler) did not believe that there was an afterlife, or a Jesus to whom they would have to give account when they died. Therefore, they felt free to use their 'absolute' power to do as they pleased, as they were ultimately answerable to no one. It is a logical consequence of atheistic politics. The State replaces God.

Incidentally, it is quite difficult to get Christianity out of a culture once it becomes deeply ingrained. Trotsky recalls that many of the early Bolsheviks thought that the movement resembled the early Christians, and had to be taught that they should be atheists. Even after generations of atheistic propaganda, Christianity in Russia still remains a significant force.

Hitchens argues that 'if religious instruction were not allowed until the child had attained the age of reason, we would be living in a quite different world.'[8] Can you see where that leads? Not to tolerance and freedom but to suppression, closing schools and banning books which do not agree with

8.   Christopher Hitchens, *God Is Not Great,* p. 225.

the atheist agenda. When their Brave New World just does not happen, atheists will just get more and more frustrated – and as they have replaced God with the State, they will seek to use the State to suppress and intimidate. We are already beginning to see tasters of that in British society where, in the name of tolerance and diversity, biblical Christianity is increasingly not tolerated, nor allowed to be part of the 'diverse' community that people say they want.

On the other hand, in cultures where biblical Christianity has thrived there is greater freedom for a diversity of views. I find it ironic that the anti-religious Christopher Hitchens preferred to move to one of the most religious countries in the world, the U.S.A., rather than stay in an increasingly secularized Western Europe. As his brother Peter pointed out, the worst place to be an atheist is in an atheist country; the best place is in a Christian country. Know the truth, and the truth will set you free.

Doesn't religion lead to evil?

It was never that difficult to see that religion was a cause of hatred and conflict, and that its maintenance depended upon ignorance and superstition. ... [9]

Religion teaches people to be extremely self-centred and conceited. [10]

---

9.   Ibid, p. 74.

10. Ibid, p. 74.

Most Western liberals see religion as the primary cause of evil and conflict. You seem to agree with the quotations from Hitchens above. I find it difficult to disagree, mainly because there is a great deal of truth in them. Religion not only is an expression of humanity's hatred, violence and selfishness, but sometimes it exacerbates and increases it. However, not all that is called religion is like that, and only the most extreme and irrational of fundamentalist atheists would state that religion 'poisons *everything*'. Hitchens does have a point, and I agree with him that 'man-made' religion does do a great deal of harm. You do realize that the Bible is far more concerned about false religion than it is about atheism? The trouble is that people will argue that *all* religions are man-made. I deny that biblical Christianity is so – and I deny that Jesus is just another god created in mankind's own image. So what is the difference? In every religion in the world, the story is of man trying to make his way up to God, through a series of rituals, good works, submissive obedience, and similar. In biblical Christianity, the story is of God reaching down to man in Jesus Christ. That's a phenomenal difference.

Once people believe in a God of justice, mercy and love – a God who will come to judge the living and the dead – then it acts not as a cause of evil, but a restraint on evil. If Stalin had believed that he would have to answer to God for his actions, then I do not believe he would have been responsible for killing thirty million Russians.

What Hitler did *not* believe and what Stalin did *not* believe and what Mao did *not* believe and what the SS did *not* believe and what the NKVD did *not* believe and what the commissars, functionaries, swaggering executioners, Nazi doctors, Communist Party theoreticians, intellectuals, Brown Shirts, Black Shirts, Gauleiters, and a thousand party hacks did *not* believe was that God was watching what they were doing ... That is, after all, the *meaning* of a secular society [11]

Christianity does the opposite of evil – it leads to a good which cannot be explained simply by natural human goodness. Matthew Parris, an atheist and the best writer in Britain, wrote an astonishing article in *The Times*. In this, he admitted that what he had seen in Malawi made him rethink his atheism, because it was Christianity which was changing people's hearts and therefore human society for the better.

Now a confirmed atheist, I've become convinced of the enormous contribution that Christian evangelism makes in Africa: sharply distinct from the work of secular NGOs, government projects and international aid efforts. These alone will not do. Education and training alone will not do. In Africa Christianity changes people's hearts. It brings a spiritual transformation. The rebirth is real. The change is good.[12]

11.   David Berlinski, *The Devil's Delusion: Atheism and its Scientific Pretensions* (New York: Basic Books, 2009), p. 26-7.

12.   Matthew Parris, 'As an Atheist, I Truly Believe Africa Needs God,' *The Times* online, 8 January, 2009.

Doesn't Christianity stifle creativity?

You ask about the way that Christianity stifles the arts and music. I am not sure I can accept that premise. In fact I would be prepared to argue the opposite. I was visiting the Metropolitan Museum of Art in New York and was astounded at the crowds in the seventeenth, eighteenth and nineteenth-century galleries – and then I went into the twentieth-century gallery. There was enough space to play five-a-side football! Why? Surely twenty-first century people would have been keener on twentieth-century art? It's a complex question, but I think that one aspect is that largely twentieth-century art lost its way, becoming a commercialized caricature of itself (and I say this as someone who likes a great deal of modern art, and supports modern art galleries). Hans Rookmaaker's *Modern Art and the Death of a Culture* traces some of the developments in this. The fact is that Christianity has always encouraged art. Jesus is supreme patron of the arts. And why not? After all, if we believe that He is God, and God is Creator, and we are created in His image, then surely that enhances rather than restricts creativity?

Christianity has always been associated with music as well. Our God is a God who sings. 'He will take great delight in you, he will quiet you with his love, he will rejoice over you with singing' (Zeph. 3:17). There have been many musicians who believe that their music was a gift from God. I remember one atheist saying that the best argument for God he had ever heard was J. S. Bach. The late great Johnny Cash expressed it well:

> And that was the first time I remember her [my mother] calling my voice 'the gift'. Thereafter she always used that term when she talked about my music, and I think she did so on purpose, to remind me that the music in me was something special given by God. My job was to care for it and use it well; I was its bearer, not its owner.[13]

I am certainly not saying that the best musicians or songwriters are always Christians; far from it. I am saying, however, that the gift of music is one of the great gifts of God. Calvin taught that of all the gifts God had given us it is the most powerful. The great themes of the Bible – creation, humanity, sin, redemption, love, life, death, beauty, ugliness and hope – are the themes out of which the best music arises. I think of a band I absolutely love, *The Manic Street Preachers.* Apart from the name (cross off the last 's' and it makes a great T-shirt slogan for me!) I love the way they explore these great themes through their music. Although at one level they come across as anti-religious, I think their analysis of the human situation is often spot on, and the questions they ask are all answered in Christ. Richey Edwards, their initial lead singer who sadly

13.   Johnny Cash, *Cash, the Autobiography* (London: HarperCollins, 1997), p. 54.

disappeared (presumed suicide), wrote, 'I never saw the point of organized religion.' In his desperate search for meaning, he tried drugs, alcohol and self-mutilation. He describes an idyllic childhood and a rotten adult life. He became obsessed with religion and the basic questions of humanity, latterly carrying a book of biblical quotes everywhere. Their album, *The Holy Bible*, unlike the real Bible, is full of pain and without any real hope.

Isn't Christianity against equality and diversity?

I love this question because everyone asks it as though it was evident what it means. But is it? Equality and diversity for whom? Words are cheap, but you shall know them by their fruits. I live in the United Kingdom where, as we are becoming more and more anti-Christian, we are becoming less equal and arguably less diverse. It seems that modern secular society cannot cope with disagreement and real diversity. On the other hand, Christianity is the most diverse, open and accepting way of life I know. I like the way that Mark Driscoll explains it.

> Jesus is both the sum and center of our Christian faith. …
> Unlike most religions, Christianity has no place, language,
> race, or culture that serves as a center to hold it together.
> Christians share no worldwide headquarters, no common
> language, no common race or ethnic heritage, and no
> common cultural framework. The only thing that holds all

of Christianity together is the risen Lord Jesus Christ who is alive today.[14]

One man who, when his wife became a Christian, went off and joined a pagan society, told me that he was very happy for his children to come to church, because 'you offer something we don't have – this is the only place I know in Dundee where people of different ages, different social backgrounds and different nationalities mix together.' You will find that the best answer to the charge of being against equality and diversity is the church.

Doesn't Christianity suffocate progress in modern medicine?
You noticed Hitchens's comment on this. 'The attitude of religion to medicine, like the attitude of religion to science, is always necessarily problematic and very often necessarily hostile.'[15] The only problem is that this is complete rubbish as regards Christianity. In fact it is very doubtful if you would have modern medicine without Christianity. The followers of Jesus Christ have always been into healing, from the early medical monks through to Florence Nightingale and the Red Cross. There is a reason why so many hospitals in the U.S.A. are religious hospitals. I suspect, though, that you were referring to the extreme examples of some Christians who believe it is wrong to seek medical help and instead prefer to

---

14.   Mark Driscoll, *Vintage Jesus* (Wheaton, Ill.: Crossway Books, 2008), p. 200.

15.   Christopher Hitchens, *God Is Not Great*, p. 47.

wait for God to heal. I have read about such but, in many years, I have never met anyone who expounds this doctrine. I believe that God can, and sometimes does, miraculously heal, but I still go to the doctor (far too frequently!) and am deeply grateful for the God-given gift of modern medicine – as I am for the many doctors, nurses and dentists in my church who serve God in their particular healing ministry.

Isn't the church full of hypocrites?

Sometimes I suspect that the main reason for a lot of people not believing in Jesus is the perceived, and actual, hypocrisy of many who profess to follow Jesus Christ. You have asked me this question as well. Now, the smart answer would be to say, 'Yes, you would feel at home.' But then, you would never get a smart answer from me, just as I would never in a million years exaggerate! Of course, it is easy to hide behind the truism that we are all to some extent hypocrites, failing to live up to the ideals we profess. But the question is really deeper than that. You are talking about people who profess one thing and then live out another; those who with their lips profess Christ, but by their actions deny Him. When I was asked this question (or is it more, *received this accusation?*) in my former church in Brora, in the Scottish Highlands, I used to respond by saying, 'Yes, you are right, but do you know any real Christians?' What astounded me was the almost inevitable answer 'Yes'. Then they would name the same people, 'Ross, Donald, Big Margaret, Wee Margaret, Angus' and others. These people were not the Mother Teresas of Brora. They were what the Bible calls 'saints': ordinary people who had come to see that their sins were forgiven, that they did not have to earn their rewards by religion or good works, but who lived imperfect lives of love, joy and service in a broken and needy world. They shone like stars.

I once visited a friend at Reading University only to discover that he was not in. His neighbour in the halls of residence was kind enough to let me wait with him until my friend returned. In the course of the conversation, we somehow got on to Jesus and the church. When I asked him if he was a Christian, he gave the lovely reply. 'Of course, how could you live next door to Ken and not become a Christian!' It doesn't always happen like that, but it certainly happens frequently enough. Many of my arguments against Christianity were blown away by meeting real Christians who did have that something extra, that *je ne sais quoi*, that x-factor. It did not take too long to discover that the x-factor is Christ.

Can I share one of my own theories here? I think that many atheists/agnostics keep themselves in their own groups, hide behind their keyboards and blogs, because they are afraid that, if they meet any Christians, their prejudices will be challenged rather than confirmed. If they can mock behind the safety of their computer screens, and filter out anything that causes

them to question, then it is so much safer. I mentioned Brora
– let me illustrate this from that wonderful village again. For
such a small village, it is amazing that is has two football
teams, the professional Brora Rangers, and the amateur Brora
Wanderers. Early in my days as a minister, since I liked football
and was in those days relatively fit, I thought I would join up
with Brora Wanderers, and take part in their training. I even
eventually managed to play on their team. One day I was
approached by a woman in the village, who asked me to stop
going to the football. Why? 'Because my husband goes, and
he's not going to go anymore if you keep going. That will do
my head in, as it's the only time he goes out the house. 'What?
Does he really hate me that much?' 'No, that's the problem. He
doesn't hate you; he hates the church. He likes you, and that is
really messing with his head.' It's easier to hate, denigrate, and
mock if you don't know and mix with the people. Inevitably,
such groups end up arguing against themselves, by making up
the arguments of their opponents. I realize that Christians can
do the same thing as well, which is why we are encouraged to
avoid that danger by getting out amongst people, loving them
by listening to them, and allowing our own preconceptions
and prejudices to be challenged.

Isn't the church dying anyway?

Ah – the good old 'death of God' argument along with its
twin, 'the death of the church' prophecy. Both have been

doing the rounds for hundreds of years, and both have continually been proved wrong. Christianity has not gone away and is not going away – despite the increasingly desperate cries of Hitchens and Dawkins trying to believe the discredited metanarrative of a declining church. The heroine in Nick Hornby's novel *How to Be Good* describes how many people see the church in Europe today.

> It all feels a long way from God … it feels sad, exhausted, defeated; this may have been God's house once, you want to tell the handful of people here, but He's clearly moved, shut up shop, gone to a place where there's more of a demand for that sort of thing.[16]

John Humphrys, in his rather weak case for agnosticism, says that churches are in decline because of 'thin services, banal choruses, poor preaching and unfriendly people'.[17] I suspect where these are present, it is little wonder that the church is in decline. But where there is depth, meaningful praise, good preaching and friendly people, the church is actually growing. Even in Europe. Did you know that hundreds of churches have been planted in France in the past decade? Why do you think the New Atheist writers have poured their books into the market? I will give them the credit of it not just being about the money. I think they are scared, because the

16. Nick Hornby, *How to Be Good* (London: Penguin, 2002), p. 187.

17. John Humphrys, *In God We Doubt* (London: Hodder and Stoughton, 2007), p. 211.

God they thought had gone, is still very much here. Richard Dawkins wrote *The God Delusion* not because of fear of 9/11, but rather because he was furious that so many of his students were theists – at one point he even mooted the idea that creationists should be banned from Oxford University.

For them it is going to get worse. As Christianity continues to grow and expand exponentially in Africa, South America and Asia, you will find a real reverse missionary effect. In fact, it has already begun; I work with Korean, African and Brazilian pastors in Scotland. Where the church is growing, it is growing amongst the young, especially those in the 20-40 age group. This is what annoys and frustrates those who believe that the church would and should inevitably die.

The death of the church has been predicted ever since its birth at Pentecost. The reason the church will not die, and the gates of hell will not prevail against it, is because of the source of its life. The church's life comes from Jesus Christ, who is its head. It is a living body, a family, a spiritual temple, founded by Christ, built on the foundation of the apostles and prophets, and enabled and equipped by the Holy Spirit to go into all the world, and to proclaim the good news that, in Jesus, God forgives sinners and brings peace. Its message will never be irrelevant nor not needed because, as a former Pope put it,

> Enmity with God is the source of all that poisons man; overcoming this enmity is the basic condition for peace in the world. Only the man who is reconciled with God can

also be reconciled and in harmony with himself, and only the man who is reconciled with God and with himself can establish peace around him and throughout the world.[18]

The reason the church has continued to prosper is because it is the fruits of the cross. Christ did not begin something that might fail when He was crucified. He cried 'It is finished!' because it was. The rest of history has been applying the fruits of the work, teaching, life, death and resurrection of Jesus. At some point that working out will end.

Yours etc.,

David

'But what about you?' he asked. 'Who do you say I am?'

Simon Peter answered, 'You are the Christ, the Son of the living God.'

Jesus replied, 'Blessed are you, Simon son of Jonah, for this was not revealed to you by man, but by my Father in heaven. And I tell you that you are Peter, and on this rock I will build my church, and the gates of Hades will not overcome it.' (Matt. 16:15-18)

---

18. Pope Benedict XVI, *Jesus of Nazareth: From the Baptism in the Jordan to the Transfiguration* (London: Bloomsbury Publishing, 2008), p. 85.

9 / MARANATHA

Nothing proves the man-made character of religion as obviously as the sick mind that designed hell, unless it is the sorely limited mind that has failed to describe heaven.

Christopher Hitchens[1]

No fire, no heroism, no intensity of thought or feeling, can preserve a life beyond the grave ... all the labours of the ages, all the devotion, all the inspiration, all the noonday brightness of human genius, are destined to extinction in the vast death of the solar system; and the whole temple of Man's achievement must inevitably be buried beneath the debris of a universe in ruins.

Bertrand Russell[2]

Dear J,

Thanks again for your reply – of course, you are right to point out the numerous holes, inconsistencies and hypocrisies in

---

1. Christopher Hitchens, *God Is Not Great* (London: Atlantic Books, 2007), p. 219.

2. Here, Bertrand Russell describes his 'unyielding despair' when contemplating the death of the universe. Bertrand Russell, *A Free Man's Worship* (Portland, Maine: Thomas Bird Mosher, 1923), p. 7.

the history of the church. But can't you see how that fits? If I were presenting to you a perfect church, it would be a myth. What I am presenting to you is the church of Jesus Christ, in all her beautified ugliness. Of course, the church is actually far worse than you think, and than she often pretends to be, but that is the whole point of the good news. At the individual level, Jesus Christ takes all our ugly clothes of sin and gives us instead His robes of righteousness. He beautifies us. It is the ultimate makeover, precisely because it is not a makeover – it is a completely cleansed and renewed person; in the words of the hymn writer, 'ransomed, healed, restored, forgiven'.

I read the following last night and thought of you. Tim Keller has described what Dick Lucas, long-time pastor at St Helen's Bishopsgate, in London, has said: in the Bible 'God does not give us a watertight argument so much as a watertight person against whom, in the end, there can be no argument.'[3] That is precisely what I am trying to do here – not provide you with a series of watertight arguments (we would go on forever if that were the case) but a series of arguments that point to a watertight person. The astonishing thing about some atheists/agnostics is that they really do believe that unless they are presented with absolute, concrete evidence then they cannot and will not believe. The reason why that

---

3.   Timothy J. Keller, *Center Church.* (Grand Rapids, Michigan: Zondervan, 2012).

is astonishing is because they think they have the capacity to stand back and determine both what the evidence should be, and evaluate perfectly whatever evidence there is. God has made us 'logos'. In other words, He has given us reason so that we can think about things. But our minds and reason are limited. Augustine recognized this when he wrote in *The City of God* about such people who demand absolute proof of everything: 'Mighty reasoners, indeed, who are competent to give the reason of all the marvels that exist!' He goes on to say something which is relevant to what we are looking at in this letter, the shape of things to come.

> If we were to say that these things were to be found in the world to come, and our sceptics were to reply, If you wish us to believe these things, satisfy our reason about each of them, we should confess that we could not, because the frail comprehension of man cannot master these and suchlike wonders of God's working; and that yet our reason was thoroughly convinced that the Almighty does nothing without reason, though the frail mind of man cannot explain the reason; and that while we are in many instances uncertain what He intends, yet that it is always most certain that nothing which He intends is impossible to Him and that when He declares His mind, we believe Him whom we cannot believe to be either powerless or false.[4]

---

4.   Philip Schaff (Ed.), *Nicene and post-Nicene Fathers: First Series, Volume II* (New York: Cosimo, Inc., 2007), p. 456.

The end of the world

You ask about Christians who are preparing for Armageddon. This is a reference to the belief that some Christians have (based on Revelation 16:16) about the last great battle on earth. I am always wary about beliefs based on only one particular verse, even more so when it comes in a difficult-to-grasp book like Revelation. Revelation belongs to a genre called apocalyptic (the Old Testament book of Daniel is in large part also from the same genre). Again, to summarize the various Christian views of the end of the world in a couple of paragraphs is almost impossible. But let's see how far we get.

The Bible teaches that, just as Jesus ascended into heaven, so He will return – not this time as a baby in a manger, but as the King to judge the whole earth. Revelation, chapter 20, speaks of the Millennium, the thousand-year reign of Christ. There are three basic understandings of that (along with numerous variations): Post-, Pre- and A-millennialism. Post-millennialists believe that the gospel age began with Pentecost and will end when Christ returns, but before He does there will be a great period (not necessarily a literal thousand years) in which there will be gospel prosperity, the Jews will be converted, and many will come into the kingdom. A-milliennialists believe that the millennium began with Pentecost and that there will be no special end-time blessing. Pre-millennialists believe that Christ will return, and then establish His thousand-year reign. It is from this latter group that we get a lot of millennial thinking in the Christian church associated with strong support for the nation state of Israel (the emergence of Israel in 1948 and the occupation of Jerusalem in 1967 are seen as a fulfilment of prophecy).

The emergence of the Christian Brethren, founded by J. N. Darby in the first half of the nineteenth century, and the Scofield Bible, had an enormous impact, especially in the U.S.A.. End-times theology remains incredibly influential (and lucrative): Hal Lindsey's *Late Great Planet Earth* sold over 35 million copies in the 1970s, and Tim LaHaye and Jerry Jenkins's *Left Behind* series have sold over 65 million copies since 1995. I grew up in that tradition and can testify that the imagery of the Rapture (when Christ returns and takes Christians up to heaven, leaving the rest of the world to get on with it) is very powerful. I recall going into a friend's house once and noticing the pan boiling over in the kitchen, the radio left on and the doors open. I did for a fleeting moment wonder if Christ had come and I had indeed been left behind! However, I have since come to see that dispensational pre-millennialism is a nineteenth-century creation, and is only one particular interpretation of the Bible, which itself is by no means clear on this. The literal and physical is not the same as the literal and figurative. Whatever one's view of the millennium (personally I think, as a Christian, you could hold any one of the three) the one thing we can all agree on is that Christ is returning as both Judge and Saviour). It is surely not right to read the U.S.A. and the U.K. into the Bible, when they are not there. However, this field does allow for all kinds of weird and wonderful speculations and all manner of eccentricities. At best, they are harmless; at worst, they can fuel fantasies which could do a great deal of harm. The doctor who told me that the British are the lost tribe of Israel (a rather bizarre heresy known as British Israelitism) is not quite on a par with those who think that Armageddon is coming, so it won't do any harm to speed it up. Poor theology in the hands of twisted minds is always a dangerous combination.

As Philip Jensen states, 'Christianity is a big story religion.' There are multiple facets to the cosmic story that it seeks to tell. Sometimes people get bogged down in the details. Sometimes they get things out of proportion. But what is plain is that there is a clear Christian view of history. It is not directly linear, as some people believe (the world is steadily getting better or steadily getting worse). The Christian view is that the world is moving from the first coming of Christ, to the second, and that history is moving in an often-cyclical pattern towards that deliberate end.

I will leave it to Justin Martyr, the early church apologist, to summarize Christian teaching about the end of the world.

He shall come from heaven with glory, accompanied by His angelic host, when also He shall raise the bodies of all men who have lived, and shall clothe those of the worthy with immortality, and shall send those of the wicked, endued with eternal sensibility, into everlasting fire with the wicked devils.[5]

Hell

Let's leave the end of the world and come on to heaven and hell. Given that I promised we would return to your earlier question about hell, perhaps that's where we should begin. I know of no subject that I would want to speak about less. It is something that has always bothered me, and continues to do so. I don't understand it and I really struggle with it. And yet I believe it, for one simple reason: Jesus taught it. As I accept that my mind and capacity to understand is limited (see Augustine's quote above), therefore I trust the understanding and teaching of Jesus. It would be a strange kind of relationship if I were to call Jesus, 'Lord', and then tell Him to change His teaching because it did not suit me at any one particular point.

So spake the Son, and into terrour changed
His countenance too severe to be beheld,
And full of wrath bent on his enemies. (John Milton)[6]

---

5.   Justin Martyr, *First Apology of Justin,* in Alexander Roberts, et al (Eds), *The Ante-Nicene Fathers: the Writings of the Fathers Down to A.D. 325, Volume I: The Apostolic Fathers With Justin Martyr and Irenaeus* (New York: Cosimo, Inc., 2007), p. 180.

6.   John Milton, *Paradise Lost,* Book VI.

What did Jesus teach? Everyone from the Jehovah's Witnesses to Christopher Hitchens wants to tell us that either Jesus did not teach about hell, or if He did, it has been terribly misunderstood. It may surprise you to know that Jesus taught more about hell than anyone else in the Bible – by a long way. Why would a loving Jesus, gentle Jesus meek and mild, give such horrific teaching? The only reason I can think of is that it is true.

> The Son of Man will send out his angels, and they will weed out of his kingdom everything that causes sin and all who do evil. They will throw them into the fiery furnace, where there will be weeping and gnashing of teeth. Then the righteous will shine like the sun in the kingdom of their Father. (Matt. 13:41-43)

> When the Son of Man comes in his glory, and all the angels with him, he will sit on his throne in heavenly glory. All the nations will be gathered before him, and he will separate the people one from another as a shepherd separates the sheep from the goats ... Then they will go away to eternal punishment, but the righteous to eternal life. (Matt. 25:31-32, 46)

Jesus taught that hell is a place of torment and fire, as these Scriptures reveal: 'They [the angels] will cast them into the fiery furnace, where there will be weeping and gnashing of teeth' (Matt. 13:42); 'Depart from me, you who are cursed, into the eternal fire ...' (Matt. 25:41). In Mark 9:48, Jesus speaks about hell, 'where their worm does not die, and the fire is not quenched.'

The bottom line is that Jesus believed that there is an afterlife. He believed that what we do, say and choose in this life determines where we will spend that afterlife. He believed that there is a judgment and that after that judgment some will spend their eternity in what we call hell. It is a place of exclusion, darkness and pain, and it is eternal. That much we know. I am not sure it is wise to speculate beyond that. Images of Dante's *Inferno*, magnificent poem though it is, do not really help. It is important not to confuse the speculations of later times with the simple and stark words of Christ.

It is also important to remember that hell is about justice. I met a man from Manchester who had grown up in a nominally Christian home but had converted to Islam. Why? Because all he ever heard about in his church was a God of love, and he wanted a God of justice, who was not going to leave sin unpunished, and who would right every wrong. Ironically, his church, who doubtless thought they were presenting a more attractive version of God, had turned him away from Jesus because they presented Him as a somewhat wet blanket who let evil go unpunished. They did not teach the Jesus of the Bible – the one whose love is beyond any human comprehension, and yet who spoke so passionately of hell.

There are Christians who believe that ultimately no one goes to hell; others believe that whilst hell is real, and lasts forever, people within hell will eventually die after suffering the punishment for their sins. The traditional view has been that hell is eternal conscious torment because those in hell keep on sinning and never repent, and so get caught in a never-ending cycle of sin and punishment. I cannot think of hell without shuddering. I believe what Jesus says and the bottom line is that I believe that God is just. I also believe that Jesus came to save us from hell and that no one needs to go there. Indeed the only people in hell are those who have chosen not to go to heaven.

For me, C. S. Lewis has been a great help in trying to understand something of heaven and hell. *The Great Divorce* is a fascinating book with lots of wonderful insights (and some things I am not too sure about). I think the following two brief extracts express much better than I can what I was trying to say earlier about people ultimately choosing hell:

> There are only two kinds of people in the end: those who say to God, 'Thy will be done,' and those to whom God says, in the end, '*Thy* will be done.' All that are in Hell, choose it. Without that self-choice there could be no Hell. No soul that seriously and constantly desires joy will ever

miss it. Those who seek find. To those who knock it is opened.[7]

The choice of every lost soul can be expressed in the words 'Better to reign in Hell than serve in Heaven.'[8]

I emphasize it again. The reason that Jesus came, and suffered such a horrendous death, was to save us from the eternal death that is hell. He is the Saviour who not only came to save us *from* hell; he also came to save us *for* heaven.

Heaven

What will heaven be like? I know this sounds strange but, even as a Christian, for a number of years I struggled with the idea of going to heaven almost as much as I struggled with the idea of going to hell. Not long after I became a Christian, I was walking along the beach at Brora in the Eastern Scottish Highlands. It was about midnight and it was a glorious and beautiful, crisp and clear night, with the full moon bouncing off the calm sea. I confessed to my companion at the time, the wonderful Bible teacher, Dick Dowsett, that I did not want to go to heaven. He smiled and asked, 'Why not'? 'Because, although I know that it is not really like this, I cannot get out of my head the images of sitting on a cloud, playing a harp, or heaven being like one

---

7.   C. S. Lewis, *The Great Divorce: A Dream* (London: Geoffrey Bles, 1946), pp. 66-7.

8.   Ibid, p. 62.

eternal church service. Then, when I look at all this beauty, I think I don't want to leave that!' Dick looked horrified. 'You really have no idea about heaven. Stop and think. Look at all this beauty and you have to realize that it is just a foretaste; it is but a shadow. What you see now will be a million times more in heaven.' That was very helpful to me, as were my wonderful Dutch friends, Cees and Mieke, who, in answer to my statement that I would like to visit Barcelona, St Petersburg and Beijing before I went to heaven, smiled and said, 'All in them that is good will be in heaven'.

One of the images that helps me to understand heaven better is that of sight. Now we see but through a glass darkly, then we shall see clearly. I heard a scientist, who was based in the Antarctic, explaining on the radio that when he stood on his small hill he could now only see a hundred miles with the naked eye, whereas when he first went to the Antarctic he used to be able to see four hundred miles. It was not that his eyes were fading, but rather that the environment was becoming more polluted. It struck me that that is a great analogy for heaven. Right now we see dimly. The pollution of sin, the incapacities of our minds and the limitations of our bodies mean that we cannot conceive what God has prepared for those who love Him in the new heavens and the new earth, without the pollution of sin. Before I sat my driving test, I had to go to get an eye test. I thought my eyes were perfect and confidently told the optician that there was nothing wrong with my eyesight. When he covered over one eye and asked me to read the top line on the board, I had to ask, 'What board?!' When he gave me glasses and I put them on, everything in the room was clearer, sharper and more in focus. I had not known that my eyesight was so bad because it had gradually deteriorated. That for me is what heaven will be like. We think just now that we can judge God, that we can tell Him what is right and wrong, and that we can even determine that He does not exist. The arrogance is breathtaking because, in reality, we are blind people shouting at the light that it does not exist. When Jesus opens our eyes we begin to see, but it is only a beginning. Throughout our lives as we draw closer to Jesus we see more and more beauty. But it is only when we get to heaven that we will really see and grasp real light, ravishing beauty and absolute perfection. Then we shall see clearly.

I met an amazing young boy from Fort William at a Christian youth football camp where I was a leader. We called him 'Bendy' because of his unique ability to twist his body. His party trick was to remove his glass eye and wave it at people. His knowledge of the Bible and God was severely limited – he thought God was Irish because the only people he had heard speak about Him had been priests from Ireland! One evening we were talking about the cross and Calvary. 'I know that,' he said, 'that's where they held the Winter Olympics' (he was, of course, thinking of Calgary in

Canada); '… see, if Jesus died so that we can go to heaven, what will it be like?' We spoke about how everything would be renewed, and there would be no more death, pain or sorrow. 'Does that mean I'll get a new eye?' On being told 'Yes,' he held both his hands up to heaven and cried out, 'Bring it on!' Indeed, we shall all receive new eyes. Then we shall see clearly.

It takes an enormous shift of mind to grasp that what we are living in just now is real but is not the ultimate reality. We are tasting, but this is not yet the banquet. Heaven is not an ethereal dream but a reality to which, in contrast, this current life I am living is but a shadow. C. S. Lewis developed and spoke a great deal about this idea of the earth as the Shadowlands.

Speaking of which, I don't know a better description of heaven than the latter part of Lewis's conclusion to the Narnia tales, *The Last Battle*.

> It was the unicorn who summed up what everyone was feeling. He stamped his right fore-hoof on the ground and neighed, and then cried: I have come home at last! This is my real country! I belong here. This is the land I have been looking for all my life, though I never knew it till now. The reason why we loved the old Narnia is that it sometimes looked a little like this. Bree-heehee! Come farther up, come farther in![9]

---

9.   C. S. Lewis, *The Last Battle* (London: HarperCollins, Kindle edition), p. 228.

What all of this has to do with Jesus is this. What makes heaven heaven is the presence of the Lamb. This is yet another term for Jesus Christ. As names are descriptive, and as He is so wonderful, it is little wonder that there are so many 'names of Christ'. The Lamb refers to the Passover Lamb from the story of the Exodus, in which a lamb was killed to provide atonement for the sins of the people. Of course, the blood of lambs, bulls and goats does not take away sin: all of the Old Testament sacrificial system is pointing forward to the one Lamb, Jesus.

It is Jesus Christ who is the joy, light and life of heaven. 'We now understand that Jesus himself is "heaven" in the deepest and truest sense of the word – he in whom and through whom God's will is done.'[10] Heaven is where Jesus is; hell is where He is not. Anyone who chooses to reject Jesus and live without Him is in effect choosing hell. As Lewis said elsewhere, 'God cannot give us a happiness and peace apart from Himself, because it is not there. There is no such thing.'

The Humanist hope

There are problems, depths and many questions in thinking about all of this. Surely that is the way you would expect it to be? When human beings try to create a heaven on earth, just

10. Pope Benedict XVI, *Jesus of Nazareth: From the Baptism in the Jordan to the Transfiguration* (London: Bloomsbury Publishing, 2008), p. 151.

think how weak and pathetic our efforts are in comparison to what God does and promises. Belinda Carlisle once sang of heaven being a place on earth. God help us if that were the case. (Come to think of it, He has helped us – that's why He sent Jesus.)

What is the Humanist hope? Bertrand Russell expressed it starkly, as I mentioned in an earlier letter: '… the whole temple of man's achievement must inevitably be buried beneath the debris of a universe in ruins'. We are a blob of carbon floating from one meaningless existence to another. In the words of Talking Heads, 'We're on the road to nowhere.'

Well we know where we're goin'
But we don't know where we've been
And we know what we're knowin'
But we can't say what we've seen
And we're not little children
And we know what we want
And the future is certain
Give us time to work it out

We're on a ride to nowhere
Come on inside
Takin' that ride to nowhere
We'll take that ride[11]

---

11. David Byrne, Tina Weymouth, Chris Frantz, Jerry Harrison (Warner/Chappell Music, Inc., 1985).

Maranatha

That is really what it all boils down to. Is our life a sad, meaningless journey from nothing to nothing? Is life as Macbeth says in his final speech?

> Life's but a walking shadow, a poor player,
> That struts and frets his hour upon the stage,
> And then is heard no more; it is a tale
> Told by an idiot, full of sound and fury,
> Signifying nothing (*Macbeth,* V.v., 24–28).

Or is there something more? Surely everything in you screams out – there is more. Bob Dylan tells of the stimulation he received from being with Bono of U2: 'Spending time with Bono was like eating dinner on a train – feels like you're moving, going somewhere'.[12] That is what this life is like. It's a journey – complete with ups and downs. For me, as a Christian, it is a joy, a feast, but it is not the final destination. We are on the road to somewhere.

That somewhere is tied up with a whole host of words and concepts – beauty, truth, love, life, justice. Two books, and the films of those books, sum up what I am trying to say. I told you in an earlier letter about the young man I buried a couple of years ago. He was a great fan of *The Lord of the Rings* movies and so the family requested that we play Annie Lennox singing *Out of The West.* It is the song at the end of

---

12.   Bob Dylan, *Chronicles,* Vol. 1 (New York, Simon and Schuster, 2004), p. 174.

189

the last of the trilogy and accompanies the ship sailing into the west. It represents death, and hope, beautifully phrased and sung. Little wonder that there was not a dry eye in the house.

> Lay down
> Your sweet and weary head
> Night is falling
> You have come to journey's end
> Sleep now
> And dream of the ones who came before
> They are calling
> From across a distant shore[13]

Whilst we are on the *Lord of the Rings*, perhaps the following quotation from it encapsulates the Christian hope of heaven.

> 'Gandalf! I thought you were dead! But then I thought I was dead myself. Is everything sad going to come untrue? What's happened to the world?'

> 'A great Shadow has departed,' said Gandalf, and then he laughed and the sound was like music, or like water in a parched land; and as he listened the thought came to Sam that he had not heard laughter, the pure sound of merriment, for days upon days without count.[14]

---

13. Annie Lennox (Universal Music Publishing Group, Warner/Chappell Music, Inc.).

14. J. R. R. Tolkien, *The Return of the King* (London: George Allen and Unwin, 2nd edition, 1966), p. 230.

Please feel free to keep asking questions – you don't find, if you don't seek!

Yours etc.,

David

> 'Do not let your hearts be troubled. Trust in God; trust also in me. In my Father's house are many rooms; if it were not so, I would have told you. I am going there to prepare a place for you. And if I go and prepare a place for you, I will come back and take you to be with me that you also may be where I am. You know the way to the place where I am going.' (John 14:1-4)

10 / MAGNIFICENT

The name of Jesus is not only light but food: it is also oil, without which all food of the soul is dry; it is salt, without whose seasoning whatever is set before us is insipid; finally, it is honey in the mouth, melody in the ear, rejoicing in the heart, and at the same time medicine. Every discourse in which his name is not spoken is without savour.

Bernard of Clairvaux[1]

That was the problem with booze and drugs, wasn't it? At some point they couldn't stop that ticking sound, the sound of certain emptiness.

Barack Obama, *Dreams From My Father*[2]

There is a God-shaped vacuum in the heart of every man which cannot be filled by any created thing, but only by God, the Creator, made known through Jesus.

Pascal, *Pensées*

---

1. Bernard of Clairvaux, *Sermons on the Song of Songs*, cited in John Calvin, *Institutes of the Christian Religion*, 2:16:1.

2. Barack Obama, *Dreams From My Father* (Edinburgh: Canongate Books, 2008), p. 96.

Dear J,

Since you are imminently setting off on your travels, I think this will be my final letter to you (for now!). Perhaps it would be better if we met up for a coffee/beer/lunch next time you are in Scotland! I am thankful for your recognition that this is such a massive subject that you do not expect me to exhaust each of the facets of our discussion. Your questions have been insightful and helpful. You and I disagree about many things, but we do so respecting one another as human beings (made in the image of God!). I know that I cannot convert you and I would not attempt to do so. The Baptist preacher C. H. Spurgeon was walking with a friend when the friend spotted a drunk man staggering along the street. 'Mr Spurgeon,' he challenged, 'isn't that one of your converts?' To which Spurgeon responded, 'It must be, it certainly was not one of the Lord's.' The Bible teaches us that it is only God who can change people's hearts, regenerate and truly convert them. That is why I have great hope for you and for anyone who reads this, because God uses means, and the primary means He uses is His Spirit taking His Word to bring people to knowledge of His Son.

You spotted something in my last letter that you misunderstood (the fault is mine because I expressed it badly). You thought I was trying to be dismissive about the book of Revelation. I wasn't, and certainly did not mean to be understood as implying that. I was just urging caution. If such a great expositor as Calvin did not preach on it because he did not understand it, perhaps some of those who are so confident that they can identify every detail should take care. Yet I love Revelation; it is, after all, part of the Word of God, and I have preached through the whole book in my time. For me, it is really a poetic book, a vision, about the triumph of Christ and His church in the midst of persecution. The clue to understanding the book is in its name. It is, as its first words say, 'the revelation of Jesus Christ'. It is not intended to obscure and cover up, but rather to reveal. It is all about Jesus, the bridegroom of the church, the King on the throne of heaven, the Lamb looking as if it has been slain, the sovereign God controlling history, the preacher calling the world to repentance, the one who comes like a thief in the night and who invites us to the greatest party of all time, the wedding feast of the Lamb.

In these letters, I have sought to show you why I am obsessed with Jesus Christ. It is not about winning an argument; it is about introducing you to the most important person who has ever lived, and who will be the most important person in your life. I believe what the Bible says when it declares that every knee will bow before Jesus. All of us will acknowledge Him as Lord either in this life or in the life to come. He invites you to come to Him now, but you need to know who He is before you can come – which is why I have burned the midnight oil, doing my best to tell you of Him. Philip Pullman in his book, *The Good Man Jesus and the Scoundrel Christ*, tries, like many others before and after, to retell the story of Jesus in a way that makes him more acceptable to twenty-first-century humanity. I have not done that. I have tried to tell you the story of Jesus as it really happened, and have presented to you the understanding of it that the church of Jesus has really held over the centuries. I don't believe that we have to present our own personal Jesus.

I accept that the story of Jesus has been obscured and covered over in so many ways: not so much in the retelling, but rather in the way that those who profess to be His followers end up using and distorting the image of Christ. Peter Kuzmic, President of the Evangelical Seminary in Osijek in the former Yugoslavia, said that 'In going out to evangelise in Yugoslavia, I frequently tell our seminary students that our main task may be simply to "wash the face of Jesus". For it has been dirtied and distorted by both the compromises of institutional Christianity through the centuries and the antagonistic propaganda of atheistic communism in recent decades.'[3] In a sense, that is what I have been trying to do – wash away some of the distortions and accretions that have accumulated over the years and that may be part of your thinking about Jesus.

---

3.   Cited in John Stott, *The Incomparable Christ* (Leicester: InterVarsity Press, 2001), p. 129.

There is a warning here, though. There is a meme in our culture that could cause you to stop and back off from any further investigation. Basically, atheism is logically untenable. To claim that one knows there is not a God is a blind statement of faith and a classic example of wishful thinking. It's why the New Fundamentalist Atheists are so emotional; because their atheism is something they feel they know, rather than something they do know. But most people are not NFAs; they are agnostics.

The claim is not only that *they* do not know, but also that *no one* can know; that the knowledge of God with any certainty is just an impossibility. The claim that Christians make about having a relationship with God is considered an absurd and delusional claim. And I will grant you that it could be. I may appear to be someone who walks around sure and certain, and who comes across as someone who has all the answers, and if I do so, I apologize – because not only is that desperately unattractive, it is also false. Like many believers, there are times that I ask myself the same questions. Have I been deluded? How do I know? How do I know that I know? The English comic Bill Bailey has a hilarious routine discussing Stephen Hawking's *A Brief History of Time*[4]. In the discussion, Bill Bailey talks about how, when he thinks about things too deeply, he goes off to

---

4.   you can get it here – http://www.youtube.com/watch?v=q-NgNvq5e_g

have a Pringle sandwich! When I get these questions, that is for me a Pringle-sandwich moment. But let's ask about how we know.

Agnosticism has the advantage of appearing both humble and intelligent. It's also quite easy because if we cannot know, there is no point in looking; let's just eat, drink and be merry, for tomorrow we die. But there are two different types of agnosticism, the foolish and the intelligent. Imagine you are sitting at home watching Barcelona v Real Madrid in the European Cup, when a man comes and knocks on your door. 'Hey mate, did you know that your house is on fire?' I can respond by telling him that I did not know (I am agnostic), and then tell him to get lost because I am in the middle of watching a great game. I don't want to be bothered by something that may not be true, and I may not know about. That is foolish agnosticism, because it is a big deal if my house burns down (an even bigger deal if I am inside it at the time). An intelligent agnostic would go to check. That is precisely what we are saying about Jesus Christ. If what the Bible says might be true, it is surely worth checking. Can there be a bigger deal than God, heaven, hell, life, beauty, truth, renewal, forgiveness and all the other themes tied in with Jesus Christ?

Sorry, I got diverted a wee bit. How do we know? In Tim Keller's *Center Church,* he talks about three ways of knowing and reasoning: the conceptual, the concrete relational and the intuitional ways. In the conceptual, we make decisions and come to beliefs through logic and analysis. In the concrete relational, decisions and beliefs are arrived at through relationships and practice. In the intuitional, they come through insight and experience. That is exactly the same with the knowledge of Jesus Christ. It is logical and can be analysed. Jesus did come in space/time history and His claims (or the claims about Him) do make sense. But to know about and to analyse in a detached way is not enough. My knowledge of Jesus comes also through the concrete relational. In that respect, the church has been vital. My relationships with other people who share the same fears and doubts, but also the same faith, have been something through which Christ has communicated Himself, as it has been with the intuitional. Insight and experience over the years has also helped in knowing Christ. As a very young Christian, I was once in the home of a group of hippies. Amidst the waft of weed, I saw a poster that had a great impact on me. It simply declared. 'All I have seen teaches me to trust the Creator for all I have not seen.' That is precisely my experience of Jesus Christ.

Keller's insight is similar to Pascal's:

There are three ways to believe: reason, habit, inspiration. Christianity which alone has reason, does not admit as its true children those who believe without inspiration. It is not that it excludes reason and habit, quite the contrary, but we must open our mind to the proofs, confirm ourselves in it through habit, while offering ourselves through humiliation to inspiration which alone can produce the real and salutary effect, lest the Cross of Christ be made of none effect.[5]

Reason, experience and revelation are essential in our knowledge of Jesus Christ.

So let's go with the advice of Socrates in Plato's *Republic* and follow the argument wherever it leads. This principle led the former atheist Antony Flew to state, 'I have followed the argument where it has led me. And it has led me to accept the existence of a self-existent, immutable, immaterial, omnipotent, and omniscient Being.'[6] He concluded, 'You cannot limit the possibilities of omnipotence except to produce the logically impossible. Everything else is open to omnipotence.'[7] We cannot automatically discount the existence of God simply on the basis that we do not feel, think or want Him to exist. A logical person will admit that the belief that the universe was created by a personal God is at least as logical as the belief that the universe self-generated out of nothing. And a reasonable person will admit that if such a God existed it would be possible to know Him if He revealed Himself.

---

5.   Blaise Pascal, *Pensées*, no. 808.

6.   Antony Flew, *There is a God* (New York: HarperCollins, 2008), p. 155.

7.   Ibid, p. 213.

The Christian position is that God has revealed Himself in two ways. His power and eternal qualities are clearly seen and understood from His creation, what the old Puritans called the book of nature. His attitude towards us, His love and His purity, are clearly seen and revealed in Jesus Christ. And how do we know Jesus? That is the purpose of the Bible, to give to us a sure and certain testimony to who Jesus is, what He did and what He continues to do.

Everyone's experience is different and I tell you my own, not to make it normative but simply because it is the one I know best, and illustrates how this basic principle of revelation works in one person's life. I was sixteen years old and trying desperately hard to be an atheist. But the trouble was I could not – because of that book of nature. My mind could not accept that everything came from nothing and that life had no beauty, purpose or meaning. But equally I despised religion and thought Christianity was hypocritical. Then one of my friends, who had had very little to do with the church, became a Christian. I was annoyed. But after a series of parties at Christmas I went with him to a small church that was having a 'watchnight' service on New Year's Eve. As I listened to the singing, reading and preaching, I was totally unconvinced, but also totally confused. When the clock came to 00:00 at midnight, I prayed simply, 'Lord, if you exist, show me and I will serve you the rest of my life.' It seemed absurd, praying to a God I was not sure existed.

I stepped out into the chill of a Highland winter's night and looked up to the heavens. There was no flash of lightning. No bolt from the blue. No angelic visitation. Nothing. Two weeks later, I was lying in bed on a Sunday morning and I just had this thought, 'I have to go to church.' I woke up my brother and told him we were going to church. He laughed. But I was older and bigger than him and suffice it to say I compelled him to come with me. Successful as it was, that is a method of evangelism that I have never used since! As we were sitting in this small church by the seaside, the waves so close that I could hear them lapping against the sea walls, everything did become clear. Of course God existed. Nothing made sense without this. Once I accepted that, it was easy to accept the good news of Jesus, because that made so much sense as well. From that moment on, I knew that the rest of my life would be the second part of my very simple prayer. And so it has proved to be. Thirty-five years later, I have had many ups and downs, doubts and fears, but this one thing has remained constant. I am a follower and lover of Jesus Christ.

You can see from my own story how the three types of knowledge – conceptual, concrete relational and intuitive – have come together. I have yet to hear anyone's story that does not include all of these. Last night, we had a great house group where three people shared how they became Christians. One was English with no religious background, one Scottish with a strict religious background that they rebelled against and one Indian with a nominal religious background. Each of them came to Jesus Christ (or He to them) in very different ways, and yet their stories, although different, were similar. That is the way it is with real Christianity. It's not like joining a social club or accepting a philosophy. It is about coming to a personal knowledge of Jesus Christ.

I am not one of those who is going to argue that my whole belief in Jesus Christ is based like the words of the old hymn, 'You ask me how I know he lives, he lives within my heart.' That would be absurd to expect you to believe on the basis of of my feeling! Like the former Pope, Benedict, I would argue that faith in God is the one thing that makes sense of the world's rationality.

> The world is now seen as something rational: It emerges from eternal reason, and this creative reason is the only true power over the world and in the world. Faith in the one God is the only thing that truly liberates the world and makes it rational.[8]

Yet it is not enough to know only in our minds – we do have to experience it as well. As Jack says to Glory, in the wonderful Marilynne Robinson novel, *Home*: 'It is possible

8.   Pope Benedict XVI, *Jesus of Nazareth: From the Baptism in the Jordan to the Transfiguration* (London: Bloomsbury Publishing, 2008), p. 174.

to know the great truths without feeling the truth of them. That's where the problem lies. In my case.' Pascal, too, wrote: 'We know the truth not only through our reason but also through our heart.'[9] Pope Benedict concurs: 'The organ for seeing God is the heart. The intellect alone is not enough.'[10] That is why I pray for God to grant you the eyes of both intellect and heart.

So let's come to the final question. Why is Jesus my *magnificent obsession*? Why does He mean more to me than everything and everyone else? I hope that the answer is clear from my previous letters, but let me summarize it here.

Jesus is the reason for my life

Look at the quote from Barack Obama at the head of this letter. What does it illustrate? The nagging, gnawing sense of emptiness that so many of us have. The sense that there has to be something more than this. Bob Geldof, together with Midge Ure, was the inspiration behind the first Live Aid concert at Wembley in 1985. He pulled off an incredible feat, getting so many major acts together, doing other concerts throughout the world, setting up Band Aid and getting an audience of some 1.9 billion. Yet, at the end, he turned to Midge Ure and said, 'Is that it?' The phrase became the title of his best-selling autobiography. It is the

---

9.   Blaise Pascal, *Pensées*, no. 110.

10.   Pope Benedict XVI, *Jesus of Nazareth* (2008), p. 92.

question we should all ask – is that it? I don't know if you have ever had the experience of achieving your stated goal and then wondering, is that it? I love how Ravi Zacharias describes the disappointment of fulfilled pleasure:

> The greatest disappointment (and resulting pain) you can feel is when you have just experienced that which you thought would bring you the ultimate in pleasure – and it has let you down. Pleasure without boundaries produces a life without purpose. That is real pain. No death, no tragedy, no atrocity – nothing really matters. Life is sheer hollowness, with no purpose.[11]

Jesus Christ brings that purpose. I am not like Bertrand Russell. I do not expect everything to fade away into oblivion. I know that what is done for Christ will last and that my brief moment on this earth has eternal significance because of Him.

The Westminster Shorter Catechism asks the question 'What is the chief end [main purpose] of man?' and answers it: 'Man's chief end is to glorify God, and to enjoy him forever.' That is a great purpose. The Westminster divines who drew this up were only passing on the teaching of Irenaeus from the second century, who explains that true life is impossible without the source of life: 'It is not possible to live apart from life, and the means of life is found in

11.   Ravi Zacharias, *The End of Reason* (Grand Rapids, Michigan: Zondervan, 2008), p. 41.

fellowship with God; but fellowship with God is to know God, and to enjoy His goodness.'[12]

Sometimes, when people hear someone like myself say Jesus is my magnificent obsession, they get a wee bit scared. They imagine I am some kind of religious fanatic for whom the only thing that matters is religion, and everything else can go to the dogs. That is not the case; in fact, precisely the opposite. If the world were simply heading for oblivion, why should anything ultimately matter? But because the world was created by and for Jesus Christ, then everything does matter. I don't love my wife less because I love Jesus more. I love her more. I don't love humanity, music, literature, nature or whisky less because I love Jesus more. I love them more. What I love less are those things that are anti-Christ – hatred, sin, evil, and the devil and his perversions of God's gifts. Julian Hardyman's *Glory Days* has the subtitle, *Living the whole of your life for Jesus*. That is the story of my life since the day I bowed the knee to Jesus.

Let me divert into one particular rabbit warren that people often bring up. Okay, they say, it's good and virtuous to be such a committed believer, but isn't it really, really boring! (I think we are back to the playing of harps on a cloud in an eternal church service.) I don't know if this can be said

---

12. Irenaeus, in Alexander Roberts, et al (Eds), *The Ante-Nicene Fathers: the Writings of the Fathers Down to A.D. 325, Volume I: The Apostolic Fathers With Justin Martyr and Irenaeus* (New York: Cosimo, Inc., 2007), p. 489.

for every Christian but, for me, I can honestly testify that, for over thirty-five years serving Jesus, I have never known a single moment of boredom. Life has been enriching, frustrating, beautiful, ugly, joyful and heartbreakingly painful. But it is never boring with Christ!

Jesus is the source of my forgiveness

No matter how I tried to escape it, I could not get away from the fact that I was born in sin, I would live in sin and I would die in sin.

> Not my vegetarian dinner, not my lime juice minus gin
> Quite can drown a faint conviction that we may be born in
> Sin (John Betjeman).[13]

Most people, if they are honest, will acknowledge that they are sinners. Hitchens is honest in this: 'If I search my own life for instances of good or fine behaviour I am not overwhelmed by an excess of choice.'[14] The trouble with the unbelief of many secular, non-religious (as well as many religious people) is that they have a profound faith in the goodness of humanity. You told me that once – that you *had* to believe that humanity was good, or life would be miserable. Gone were the demands for empirical evidence; you just had to believe it. But as a historian and an observant human being, I cannot accept

13.   John Betjeman, 'Huxley Hall'.
14.   Christopher Hitchens, *God Is Not Great* (London: Atlantic Books, 2007), p. 188.

that faith. I know that the world is screwed up and I know something of my own heart: I am screwed up too. We are lost. 'Why do we presume so much on the ability of human nature? It is wounded, battered, troubled, lost. What we need is true confession, not false defence.'[15]

Some people will see this but then think that we can save ourselves. That is impossible. Remember the 'challenge' I set before you in chapter 4 on page 86? How did you get on? Do you think it can be done? So we seek 'functional saviours' from elsewhere. Some seek solace in substance abuse; some seek power and politics; some look for entertainment and excitement; some obtain work and wealth; some find family and friends; some even go in for religion and ritual. Yet none of it is enough. So am I doomed to 'get no satisfaction'?; Is that it? I need forgiveness, redemption, to know that I am forgiven so that I can forgive. I need a new heart so that I can see God. 'Blessed are the pure in heart, for they will see God' (Matt. 5:8). And that new heart is only ultimately found in Jesus Christ.

When I look at my sins (and if I think they're sins, then they are sins), I can see the appeal of born-again Christianity. I suspect that it's not the Christianity that is so alluring; it's the rebirth. Because who wouldn't wish to start all over again?[16]

15. John Calvin, *Institutes of the Christian Religion*, 2:11:11.

16. Nick Hornby, *How to Be Good* (London: Penguin, 2002), p. 181.

As this is my last letter, let me anticipate one objection that you may have to this. You know me. You know that, despite being a Christian, I still have faults, I still sin. I admit this completely. I am not claiming that I no longer sin, nor that knowing Christ has removed from me all trace of sin (yet!). I am still a sinner. In fact, knowing my own heart, I would go further and say as Paul did, that 'I am the chief of sinners.'[17] But here is the difference. When I ask – as Paul did – 'Who will rescue me from this body of death?'[18] I can relax and rejoice with the wonderful answer 'Jesus Christ'.

Jesus is my freedom

This is the consequence of forgiveness. I have freedom – from fear, from the consequences of sin, from the devil, from self, from the tyranny of society. We are all desperate for freedom. Rousseau's famous saying, that 'Man is born free; but everywhere he is in chains,' is only half correct. We are not even born free, and we certainly are in chains. The Bible's contention is that we are freed, and only are freed, through Jesus Christ. Augustine stated that the human will does not obtain grace by freedom, but obtains freedom by grace. It is only by knowing the truth that we can be set free. The Bible's claim is that that truth is found in a person – Jesus Christ.

---

17. See 1 Timothy 1:15.

18. Romans 7:24.

Jesus Christ is my hope for the future

I believe that as a Christian I am freed from the power and penalty of sin. One day I will be freed from the presence of sin, both internally and externally. Jesus is my hope. When I debated in London with the architect of the Government's policy on same-sex marriage, we both received a wonderful question from a West Indian man in the audience. 'What is your hope?' My political opponent spoke of his hope being to see the level at which income tax was charged being raised to £10,000. I spoke of my hope in Christ, which got a spontaneous round of applause from the West Indian contingent in the audience! Actually the best way I can put it is in the wonderful words of the first question of the Heidelberg Catechism.

What is your only comfort in life and in death?

That I am not my own,
but belong body and soul,
in life and in death
to my faithful Saviour, Jesus Christ.
He has fully paid for all my sins with his precious blood,
and has set me free from the tyranny of the devil.
He also watches over me in such a way
that not a hair can fall from my head
without the will of my Father in heaven;
in fact, all things must work together for my salvation.

Because I belong to him,
Christ, by his Holy Spirit,
assures me of eternal life.

Or I can use Calvin's wonderful summary of what we receive
in Christ.

> For in Christ he offers all happiness in place of our misery,
> all wealth in place of our neediness; in him he opens to us
> the heavenly treasures that our whole faith may contemplate
> his beloved Son, our whole expectation depend upon him,
> and our whole hope cleave to and rest in him.[19]

Jesus Christ is my proof that God both exists and is good

If Bertrand Russell were able to ask God his question, 'Why
did you not give sufficient evidence?', all that God need do
is point to Jesus Christ. He is the evidence both that God
does exist and that He is love. 'What, then, shall we say in
response to this? If God is for us, who can be against us?
He who did not spare his own Son, but gave him up for us
all—how will he not also, along with him, graciously give us
all things?' (Rom. 8:31-32). Nothing can separate us from
the love of Christ. Marcus Brigstocke, in his book about his
search for God, expressed the desire for God beautifully:

> I want a personal God who loves us all in a way that goes
> beyond words. A God who fills us with a sort of reassuring

---

19.   John Calvin, *Institutes of the Christian Religion*, 3:20:1.

and magical light. A God who is the very expression of love so perfect that to feel all of it at once would be to lose yourself for ever in a place of sublime happiness.[20]

That describes Jesus perfectly. I would love for you (and Marcus) to be able to go beyond that wistful desire to certainty. What I'm saying is that's where the evidence points, and I'm not so much trying to convince you, as to effect an introduction.

Jesus Christ is my everything

He is the fountain of all true knowledge. As Calvin says, 'Outside Christ, there is nothing worth knowing, and all who by faith perceive what he is like have grasped the whole immensity of heavenly benefits.'[21] It goes beyond irony, and enters the realm of quite unbelievable sadness, that those who reject a Christ they do not know, because they think they are too knowledgeable and clever, are rejecting the source and meaning of all true knowledge and intelligence.

Jesus Christ is my identity

'I am not, in my natural state, nearly so much of a person as I would like to believe: most of what I call "me" can be very easily explained. It is when I turn to Christ, when I give myself up to His Personality, that I first begin to have a real

---

20. Marcus Brigstocke, *God Collar* (London: Transworld Publishers, 2011), p. 54.

21. John Calvin, *Institutes of the Christian Religion,* 2:15:2.

personality of my own' (C. S. Lewis).[22] I realize it can come across as very offensive to be told that we are not real, or that we do not have a real personality. When told he was missing part of his humanity by rejecting God, the director of the British Humanist Society was somewhat miffed! But think about it. If we are made for God, if we are made in God's image, if, as Augustine says, 'we are made for You and our hearts are restless until they find their rest in You,' if we are, as Paul says, 'dead in our sins and trespasses', then we really are missing something vital when we keep God away. If we leave Jesus out of the equation, are we really able to count? At a Costa coffee shop in Chelmsford, I had just finished giving a talk when an atheist stood up and asked me a great question. (I knew he was an atheist because he had a T-shirt with a big A on it!) 'Who do you think you are?' I responded by asking, 'What do you mean? Are you suggesting that because I am not an Oxford don, or a Cambridge professor, but just a simple Presbyterian pleb from Scotland, that I am not worthy of debating? Or are you asking me a more esoteric question?' He laughed and said, 'The latter. You are just one of six billion people on a tiny planet in the midst of a vast universe.' It was a great question, and I finished the evening with this answer: 'You are right. In your atheistic philosophy, I am nothing. I am, according to Bertrand

---

22.   C. S. Lewis, *Mere Christianity* (1952), Book 4, Chapter 11.

Russell, just a blob of carbon floating from one meaningless existence to another. But in the Christian understanding of the world, I am someone whom the Son of God loved and gave Himself for. My life outside of Christ has very little meaning; but in Christ it means everything.' He told me at the door that he thought it was a great answer, if only it were true. It is. My identity is found in Jesus Christ – the Christ I have been telling you about in these letters, and the Christ who is there.

I have greatly enjoyed this correspondence and I hope the feeling is at least in some measure mutual. But it is time to end. Thanks for taking the time to write. You have helped me to think through some things and to re-examine others. However, the purpose of this correspondence has not just been to provide mental stimulus for both of us. It is much more. I hope it has helped us understand one another better. But understanding is not enough either. As Grotius said: 'By understanding many things, I have accomplished nothing.'[23]

But most of all I have this hope that these letters will be used by Jesus Himself to enable you to see who He is, and to commit yourself to following Him. The apostle Paul once faced a lot of questions from a king called Agrippa. After Paul had given his defence, citing the Bible and his own personal experience of Jesus, he challenges Agrippa.

---

23.   Hugo Grotius, cited in Anna Beer, *Milton* (London: Bloomsbury, 2008), p. 92.

Then Agrippa said to Paul, 'Do you think that in such a short time you can persuade me to be a Christian?' Paul replied, 'Short time or long—I pray God that not only you but all who are listening to me today may become what I am, except for these chains'. (Acts 26:28-29)

You might be thinking just the same thing – 'Do you honestly think that, after such a short correspondence, you can persuade me to be a Christian?' I do pray that you would become what I am (a follower of Jesus), except for my sins, faults and weaknesses. If you are not at the place where you can honestly commit to Jesus, can I suggest that you keep on looking and that you pray and ask Him to reveal Himself . He does, after all, promise that those who seek Him shall find Him.

If you are ready to commit your life to Jesus, whilst I don't like formulaic prayers, can I suggest the following as an aid to prayer for you?

Lord Jesus Christ,
there are many things I do not understand,
grant me your light;
there are many things I fear,
grant me your love;
there are many sins I have committed,
grant me your forgiveness;
take my life,
all that I am,
all that I have,

all that I dream;
and create in me a new life,
a new spirit,
a renewed mind.
Baptize me with your Holy Spirit,
create in me a clean heart,
forgive my sin;
welcome me into your church,
your family,
your bride.
From now on enable me to live as your child
seeking your kingdom,
serving your people,
saving your world;
and when my time is come,
take me to be with you
in the new heavens and the new earth;
where suffering, sin and sorrow,
shall be no more.
For Jesus' sake
Amen.

If you have come to know Christ, or want to come to know Christ, then bear in mind how important the church is to help you develop that relationship.

Christians commonly say they want a relationship with Jesus, that they want to 'get to know Jesus better'. You will never be able to do that by yourself. You must be deeply involved in the church, in Christian community, with strong relationships of love and accountability. Only if you are part of a community of believers seeking to resemble, serve and love Jesus will you ever get to know him and grow into his likeness.[24]

If you want to find a good biblical church, then drop me a line and I will see what I can find. Better yet, we can discuss it in person when you get here. I leave you with an ancient wish,

I can wish no better thing for you, sirs, than this, that, recognising in this way that intelligence is given to every man, you may be of the same opinion as ourselves, and believe that Jesus is the Christ of God.[25]

Yours in Christ,

David

He then brought them out and asked, 'Sirs, what must I do to be saved?' They replied, 'Believe in the Lord Jesus, and you will be saved—you and your household.' (Acts 16:30-31)

---

24. Timothy Keller, *The Prodigal God* (London: Hodder and Stoughton, 2008), p. 127.

25. Justin Martyr, *Dialogue with Trypho*, in Alexander Roberts, et al (Eds), *The Ante-Nicene Fathers: the Writings of the Fathers Down to A.D. 325, Volume I: The Apostolic Fathers With Justin Martyr and Irenaeus* (New York: Cosimo, Inc., 2007), p. 270.

CONCLUSION /
FINAL LETTER TO THE READER

Faith of that sort – the sort that can stand up at least for a while in a confrontation with reason – is now plainly impossible.

Christopher Hitchens[1]

... too lonely to live, and too frightened to die.

Douglas Coupland[2]

Dear Reader,

Thank you for reading this far (assuming that you are not the sort of person who reads the conclusion of a book first!). I hope that you have enjoyed reading this book – even if you don't agree with everything. We began by talking about the

---

1.   Christopher Hitchens, *God Is Not Great* (London: Atlantic Books, 2007), p. 63.

2.   Douglas Coupland, *Eleanor Rigby* (London: HarperCollins, 2005), p. 247.

question of evidence, and my purpose has been achieved if you at least can see that Christians believe what we believe, not because we have a perverse belief that you should trust in the absence of evidence, but quite the reverse, precisely because there is evidence for the existence and knowability of Jesus Christ.

We do need to recognize that none of us approach this with a completely blank slate, having a completely open mind free of any prejudice or bias. We are incapable of even seeing, never mind judging, all the evidence. As I have sought to show, it is not just our minds, but also our hearts, that are involved in this. Emotion and experience, just as much as reason, play a significant part in how we come to our beliefs (and unbeliefs!). Whilst there are genuine seekers who have real intellectual questions, my experience has been that many atheists or agnostics are primarily driven by emotional rather than rational reasons. I will never forget the look on the face, the body language and the tone of the retiring president of an atheist society who, after an evening in which he saw two Christians present compelling evidence for God, turned to them and, in his last words as president, said: 'Even if you provided proof for God, I would not worship him.' It was the bitterness and venom in the tone which betrayed that this was much more a heart than a head issue.

In 2007, just after I had finished the manuscript of *The Dawkins Letters,* I experienced a couple of very strange nights

– I received a large amount of hostile comments and abuse on the Dawkins website, and felt a strong sense of heaviness and oppression. As I sat down to write the conclusion of this little book you now have in your hands, the same thing happened. It was 27 April 2013, and as I was sitting writing, Ricky Gervais, the comedian who uses his fame and media profile to push an aggressive form of atheism, tweeted me. We exchanged several tweets about the subject of this book, the evidence for Jesus, during which he said that what I was saying was 'twaddle'. From that point, every couple of minutes my phone beeped to let me know of another tweet from an irate atheist/follower of Ricky Gervais (he has 4.5 million followers). These tweets tended to refer to my lack of intelligence, evidence, sanity and goodness, and to rejoice that one day all the followers of Jesus Christ will become like followers of Ricky Gervais. The hubris, arrogance and ignorance were matched only by the emotive and angry language. Why are people so angry about a God they do not believe in? The motto of the New Fundamentalist Atheists seems to be, 'There is no God, and I hate Him'! If that is your feeling, all I can do is ask you to stop and to think about why you feel like that.

On the other hand, if you have read this book because you are genuinely curious, I want to encourage you to keep looking. I hope that you can see that this is much, much more than an academic or intellectual exercise. It is about the whole of life. Our life. Your life. The singer Lily Allen talks honestly about the culture of which she is part:

> I do feel really passionate about celebrity culture, because I hate it, I really despise it – even though I'm such a part of it. Just because I think it's so vacuous and awful. There is just nothing good comes out of it except materialism and it's horrible. It's now become like the politics of our age, that's what young people are now interested in. Kids don't read newspapers, they don't educate themselves in any way, they are reading [celebrity stories] and that's what they are getting riled up about. That's what depresses me because it bears no relevance to anyone's life at all.[3]

The story of Jesus is not a celebrity story. It is not about idle gossip. It is about the very source and purpose of life itself. It is the most relevant story of all.

Christopher Hitchens was incredibly arrogant to claim that the war against faith had been won. In fact, his statement that faith was now impossible smacked more of desperation than truth. It is one of the reasons that the New Atheists are called fundamentalists. I don't use that name just to wind them up (that would be too easy – and probably not very Christian!); I use it because it is true. The New Atheists have a series of beliefs that are fundamental to their identity, for

---

3.   'Best of British: Breakfast with Lily Allen' in *The Spectator* (Dec. 2008), p. 24. http://www.spectator.co.uk/features/3088676/best-of-british-breakfast-with-lily-allen/.

which they have no evidence and which they do not dare question. For this reason, they get extremely emotional and angry when you question them. They believe that, (apart from religion) humanity is basically good, that they are the progressive ones, that science and faith are opposed, that faith is the opposite of evidence, that miracles cannot happen and – probably the most fundamental and circular reasoning of all – they demand that you show them evidence for God, whilst at the same time believing that no such evidence can possibly exist, with the result that any evidence you do show them is automatically considered inadmissible. They then engage in constant confirmation bias, following their own blogs, being reassured by tweets of the famous who share their prejudices, and joining in the mockery of the self-evidently deluded (i.e., anyone who does not agree with them).

I am, of course, aware that the same charge can be made against many Christians, with at least a degree of truth. Except that if we really are Christians, we are called by Christ to be humble, to realize that we do not know it all, and that we are to love those who are opposed to us. And loving includes listening to, and seeking to understand, different points of view. That is why I try to read atheist, agnostic and other religious works – so that I can question my own faith, understand others and am better able to communicate. I admit that I have had many doubts about many things, but I constantly come back to the one person who just won't let me go. My magnificent obsession, Jesus Christ. The Jesus that loves us, and the love that He displays, is more magnificent and wonderful than any words can absolutely convey. To know the love that surpasses knowledge is the mystery and wonder of the Christian faith.

Please do not fall for the New Atheist lie that faith is belief that is in spite of, and contrary to, the evidence. That is their definition, not the standard dictionary definition (at least up until the twenty-first century) and, most importantly, not the Christian definition of faith. Surely it is common sense to argue against what your opponents are saying, rather than what they are not saying, or what you wish they were saying. When Richard Dawkins asked me about this at the Stornoway book festival, he described faith as being, 'I believe it because I believe, because I believe,' and then said that his position was 'belief based upon evidence'. As I pointed out, his latter statement was the Christian position, not his straw-man definition of Christian faith. We believe in Jesus because of the evidence.[4] True faith is based on knowledge, knowledge of Christ. As Calvin defines it, it is faith that rests upon the knowledge of Christ. 'Now we shall possess a right definition of faith if we call it a firm and certain knowledge of God's benevolence toward us, founded upon the truth

---

4. You can see the exchange here – http://www.youtube.com/watch?v=vUv7sYBXEFw.

of the freely given promise in Christ, both revealed to our minds and sealed upon our hearts through the Holy Spirit.'[5]

Fergus Stokes, a humanist and psychotherapist, and a former Baptist minister, was very critical of the kind of thing that I have been doing in this book. Speaking on the BBC Radio 4 programme, *Beyond Belief* on 24 August 2009, he opined: 'Evangelism is an evil – sells people surrogate answers and false solutions.' That is not what has been done here. Evangelism is telling people the good news about Jesus (from the Greek word 'evangelion' – to announce good news). By definition, surrogate answers and false solutions are not good news. When asked about his alternative 'good news', and the way humanists evangelize, he avoided the question: 'We don't spend a lot of time trying to persuade adults that there isn't a Santa Claus, or a tooth fairy. People with a mature and developed understanding of life de-evangelize themselves.' You see what he has done? Fergus Stokes equates belief in Jesus with Santa Claus or the tooth fairy, despite the fact that no adult believes in those, and he plays the Emperor's-new-clothes card – if you are mature and developed then you won't believe this nonsense. The trap that so many fall into is that they believe this assertion without any evidence sufficient to destroy the case for Jesus Christ (indeed, contrary to the evidence that establishes it) and, desiring to

---

5.   John Calvin, *Institutes of the Christian Religion*, 3:2:7.

be thought wise, they become fools, and deny the existence of the God who created them, and the Christ who can give them new life. Fergus Stokes also fails to give the secular humanist version of good news which is neatly summed up in the atheist bus slogan campaign: 'There's probably no god, now stop worrying and enjoy life.' It's a wonderful slogan because it shows the emptiness of atheist thinking. Imagine a young mum who has just lost her child seeing that bus slogan. Do you really think that she is going to say 'Eureka! That's it. There is no God. Now I can stop worrying and just get on with life.' The slogan misses the somewhat crucial point of actually asking, 'What is life?' For some people, life is hellish, for some it is very short, for many it is meaningless. For secure, wealthy, middle-class Western liberals it can be very enjoyable, for now. But ultimately, without God, all life is vanity and meaningless. We are too lonely to live and too frightened to die. Just read Solomon's fantastic reflections on this in the book of Ecclesiastes.

My version of the bus slogan would be, "Jesus is for real. Come to him and live life to the max!" It's not a sugared drink that gives you that life, it's Christ. The Christ who invites all who are weary and heavy laden to come and get rest. That has been my purpose in this book. I hope it has been of some benefit to you.

As with *The Dawkins Letters,* the sources of this book are too numerous to mention, so I won't. Neither will

I repeat (unless to stress importance) the books I listed at the conclusion of *The Dawkins Letters,* but I would like to recommend the following for further reading and reflection.

Throughout these letters I have interacted with Christopher Hitchens's *God is not Great.* Hitchens was a wonderful writer, and there is something incredibly sad about his last book, *Mortality,* written just before he died. His statement that he did not have a body, he was a body, made in that book, is one of the bleakest faith statements I have ever found. If you want a contrast, then try reading any work by his brother, Peter. There are now many Christian writers who are attempting to refute the New Atheist attacks. Dinesh D'Souza's direct response to Hitchens, *What's so Great about Christianity,* is full of good arguments and information, but I find that it misses the main point. Far better are books like Tim Keller's *The Reason for God,* or David Glass's *Atheism's New Clothes.* Antony Flew's renunciation of his atheism, *There is a God,* is as effective a counter to the New Atheist arguments as any. Robert L. Reymond's *Faith's Reasons for Believing* has several chapters which go into far greater detail on some of the issues covered in these letters.

I have also interacted with Bertrand Russell's *Why I am not a Christian: And Other Essays on Religion and Related Subjects.* He remains remarkably influential. Solas CPC has just co-published a book with Christian Focus, *Why I am Not an Atheist,* which refutes many of the arguments contained in Russell. John Humphrys wrote a book on why he was an agnostic, not an atheist, *In God We Doubt.* It is useful only insofar as it shows just how confused people can get when they don't actually bother to listen to what Jesus said!

There are many general books on Jesus, some more helpful than others. Amongst the latter I would suggest Ravi Zacharias, *Jesus Among Other Gods*; Mark Driscoll and Gerry Breshears's *Vintage Jesus*; Peter Jensen's *The Future of Jesus,* and John Dickson's wonderful *Life of Jesus.* Robert D. Culver's, *The Earthly Career of Jesus, the Christ,* is a chronological, geographical and social account.

For the historicity of the Bible, and the reliability of the New Testament, have a look at Richard Bauckham's, *Jesus and the Eyewitnesses* and F. F. Bruce's, *The New Testament Documents, Are they Reliable?* John Dickson's *The Christ Files: How Historians Know What They Know About Jesus* is a great summary of the current position. E. P. Sanders's *The Historical Figure of Jesus* gives a great deal of data on the evidence for Jesus. In his book, *Did Jesus Exist?* Bart Ehrman – no friend of Christianity – deals with the revisionism of people who want to rewrite history so that Jesus is completely brushed out. The best popular introduction to the trustworthiness of the Bible is Amy Orr-Ewing's, *Why Trust the Bible?*

C. S. Lewis on *Miracles* brilliantly overshadows David Hume's *An Enquiry Concerning Human Understanding.* Hume is the prophet of twenty-first-century sceptics who seem to believe he has had the last word. B. B. Warfield's *Miracles,* and his *The Emotional Life of our Lord,* are deep but stimulating. John Lennox's *God's Undertakers: Has Science buried God?* deals with the false dichotomy which tells us that science and faith are opposed.[6] There are many books about the teaching of Jesus. Again, I have found anything by F. F. Bruce to be helpful, especially his *Hard Sayings of Jesus.* I mention, but would not recommend, Steve Chalke's *The Lost Message of Jesus.* Only read it if you want to get lost. Far better to go to Philip Ryken's *Loving the way Jesus Loves,* to get a real glimpse into the depth and love of Christ.

John Stott's *The Cross of Christ,* Tim Keller's *King's Cross* and, strangely enough, John Bunyan's classic, *The Pilgrim's Progress,* are great at helping us understand what is the biblical teaching about the cross. Rob Bell's *Love Wins* is not helpful at all. It undermines the biblical teaching and waffles its way rather badly round church history, theology and philosophy. Far better than Bell's nineteenth-century Protestant liberalism in twenty-first century evangelical guise is the nineteenth-century Scottish writer Hugh Martin's devotional work, *The Shadow of Calvary.* Despite the dated language, it is a beautiful and moving meditation which shows what love winning really means.

---

6.   You can also find an excellent talk by Lennox on this subject at http://www.
      bethinking.org/resurrection-miracles/intermediate/the-question-of-miracles-the-
      contemporary-influence-of-david-hume.htm.

N. T. Wright's magnum opus *The Resurrection of the Son of God* is as detailed, scholarly and convincing an account as you are going to get. I love the practical applications of Sam Alberry's *Lifted: Experiencing the Resurrection Life* and the simple but powerful apologetic of Michael Green's *The Day Death Died.*

Mike Reeves's *The Good God,* and Donald Macleod's *Shared Life* are the best popular introduction to the doctrine of the Trinity. Macleod's *Jesus is Lord: Christology Yesterday and Today* manages to be both scholarly and devotional. For understanding what the Bible means when we talk about God, I find it hard to beat J. I. Packer's enduring classic, *Knowing God.* John Stott's *The Incomparable Christ* gives great insight into the Christ of Scripture, Christ through the ages and the returning Christ.

In terms of church history, I would like to recommend the excellent series by Nick Needham, *2000 Years of Christ's Power,* and three superb books by Mike Reeves, *The Breeze of the Centuries, The Unquenchable Flame* and *On Giants' Shoulders.* These are general popular introductions. There are many other books, which go into greater depth, and there are many primary source materials. As you will see from the number of quotes, I love reading the early Church Fathers, Augustine and Calvin. Augustine's *Confessions* and Calvin's *Institutes* are two of the most influential books in the history of mankind, and deserve to be read by every educated person! You are spoilt for riches. *The Ante-Nicene Fathers* and *The Nicene and Post-Nicene Fathers* book sets look good in your library but, more than that, they repay detailed study. I read ten pages per day and find them to be wonderfully stimulating.

You will forgive me for mentioning my own *Awakening: the Life and Ministry of Robert Murray McCheyne,* which shows how, in classic biblical Christianity, theology, social justice, evangelism and love of Jesus all go together. Other history books that have taught me His Story include Antonia Fraser's *Cromwell: Our Chief of Men*; Christopher Hill's *The World Turned Upside Down;* and Tim Jeal's *Stanley: The Impossible Life of Africa's Greatest Explorer.*

Rather than relying on quote-mining from selected speeches of Hitler, I would suggest reading any of the standard reference works on Hitler and the Nazis. If you want a detailed refutation of the argument that Hitler was a Christian read Joseph Keysor's *Hitler, the Holocaust and the Bible.* Traudl Junge (Hitler's secretary) wrote a fascinating account, *Until the Final Hour,* which also helps explode that myth. Simon Sebag Montefiore's *Stalin: the Court of the Red Tsar,* and *Young Stalin* are fascinating.

As well as Calvin and Augustine you will note the frequent occurrences of quotes from Pascal's *Pensées* and Pope Benedict's trilogy on *Jesus of Nazareth.* There are some people who express surprise and even disappointment that

I love the latter's books. I'm afraid they will have to be disappointed. I follow Flew's maxim that we go where the facts lead us and, although there are some things I would disagree with, I find the Pope's books to be scholarly, biblical and Christ-centred. Highly recommended.

On heaven and hell, C. S. Lewis's *The Great Divorce,* as well as his *The Last Battle,* are thought-provoking. Edward W. Fudge and Robert A. Peterson's *Two Views of Hell* and Ajith Fernando's *Crucial Questions about Hell* cover much of the ground.

Some biographies I found helpful were Barack Obama's *The Audacity of Hope* and *Dreams from my Father;* Simon Price's *Everything* (a book about the Manic Street Preachers)*;* Steve Stockman's *Walk On: The Spiritual Journey of U2;* Bob Dylan's *Chronicles, Volume One; and* Johnny Cash's *Cash: The Autobiography.*

Whilst not a biography, Thomas à Kempis's *The Imitation of Christ* is a devotional classic with some wonderful gems (and some hidden traps – beware, it could drive a sensitive soul into an overdoze of guilt!). And, finally, Tim Keller's *The Prodigal God* is a book I feel I could give almost anyone and they would find it helpful.

I find fiction can also be a vehicle for truth and for helping think through things. If you want a good laugh, read Dan Brown's *Da Vinci Code*. It will also help you see where some of the modern atheist myths spring from – really badly written fiction! Well-written fiction, but appalling theology, comes from Philip Pullman's *The Good Man Jesus and the Scoundrel Christ.* Tolstoy's *Anna Karenina* is a thought-provoking work which is not just about love and marriage, but about the search for God. Others include Marilynne Robinson's *Home,* Nick Hornby's *How to be Good,* Hilary Mantel's *Bring up the Bodies,* Douglas Coupland's *Eleanor Rigby,* Ian McEwan's *Atonement,* Dostoevsky's *The Idiot,* and the book that surely everyone has read by now, J. R. R. Tolkien's *The Lord of the Rings.*

I read a lot of magazines (hardly any newspapers, as most seem to have given up on the concept of news) but especially *Prospect, The Spectator* and *Tabletalk.* There are numerous websites which have been helpful. For answering questions and provoking thought, these four should help: http://www. bethinking.org , Solas , RZIM and Fixed Point Foundation.

For further investigation, we have found that attending a course like *Christianity Explored* really helps (http://www. christianityexplored.org/course). John Dickson's *Life of Jesus* course is less well known but is an absolute gem. Setting Jesus in the historical context really helps the modern mind come to grips with the reality of Christ and clear the mind of the cobwebs of religious mythology.

There are numerous podcasts as well: *Unbelievable,* with Justin Brierly, John Dickson's Centre for Public Christianity,

RZIM and Matt Chandler's, all provide stimulus through headphones!

I learn a lot from films. Malick's *The Tree of Life* and *To the Wonder* are stunningly beautiful; *Babette's Feast, The Passion of the Christ, The Shawshank Redemption* and *The Lord of the Rings* trilogy are the movies to accompany this book.

As for the soundtrack: Hans Zimmer's *Gladiator,* Leonard Cohen's wonderful *Old Ideas,* U2's *The Joshua Tree,* Robert Plant and Alison Krauss, Mumford & Sons, the Manic Street Preachers, Bach, the psalms of Sons of Korah, the hymns of Keith and Kristyn Getty, and the spiritual rap of Lecrae. Sons of Korah's version of Psalm 91 has become the theme tune of my life since my near-death experience in hospital!

If you like poetry, I would like to recommend the poems of G. K. Chesterton and John Milton's *Paradise Lost,* which I would regard as the greatest poem ever, if it were not for the book of Job! Speaking of Job, as I finish this book I am also preparing a sermon for Sunday on the book of Job. As it happens, we are coming to these well-known words:

> I know that my Redeemer lives,
>> and that in the end he will stand upon the earth.
> And after my skin has been destroyed,
>> yet in my flesh I will see God;
> I myself will see him
>> with my own eyes—I, and not another.
>> How my heart yearns within me! (Job 19:25-27)

I long for all of you to have that certain knowledge of Christ. That is why the last book I want to recommend is one that many people talk about, and have an opinion about, and think they know what it teaches – but they rarely read it. The Bible. The sixteenth-century scholar and Reformer, Erasmus, wrote: 'The Bible will give Christ to you, in an intimacy so close that he would be less visible if he stood before your eyes.'[7] Read the Bible!

Let me return to Ricky Gervais. He is a comedian and in today's society stand-up comedians are the prophet-preachers of our generation. They stand on the stage, six feet above contradiction and though they claim to be radical and offensive, in reality they give the audience what the audience have paid to hear. I have spent far too much time listening to Jimmy Carr, Frankie Boyle, Bill Bailey, Reginald D. Hunter, Billy Connolly and George Carlin. Witty, perceptive, crude and lewd, the one target they seem to have in common is religion in general and Christianity in particular. Why? Are they really looking for some meaning and expressing their search, fears and anger through comedy? If you want to understand more of this, I can highly recommend Marcus Brigstocke's *God Collar*, a book largely about his search for God. And if you want to hear an unusual comedian (because he is both funny and a Christian) google Tim Vine, and you will get a different perspective!

---

7. Cited in John Stott, *The Incomparable Christ* (Leicester: Inter-Varsity Press, 2001), p. 15.

Ricky Gervais asked me about the evidence for God. When I told him that I was writing this book precisely about that subject, he suggested that if I had proof of Jesus Christ, then it would be the greatest scientific discovery ever, and I would deserve the Nobel prize. Even allowing for the fact that he is confused about the whole question of evidence, I am really looking forward to my Nobel prize! But for me, a far greater prize would be if anyone came to believe because of what they read here. I pray for you all. Mr Gervais is at the top of my prayer list as well. The church could do with a few more comedians and a few less clowns!

I conclude with a story told by Donald Coggan, former Archbishop of Canterbury.

> There was a sculptor once, so they say, who sculpted a statue of our Lord. And people came from great distances to see it. Christ in all his strength and tenderness. They would walk all around the statue, trying to grasp its splendour, looking at it now from this angle, now from that. Yet still its grandeur eluded them, until they consulted the sculptor himself. He would invariably reply. 'There's only one angle from which this statue can be truly seen. <u>You must kneel.</u>'[8]

We bow in worship and acknowledge Jesus is Lord!

Yours in him,

David.

---

8.   Cited in John Stott, Ibid, p. 251.

P. S.

This book is dedicated to the memory of David Jack, a fine young medical student who tragically collapsed and died as he finished his degree. David was an inspiration in his character, lifestyle, relationships and love for the Lord. He too shared my 'magnificent obsession'.

Any author nowadays seems obliged to act like an Oscar winner and thank everyone they have any connection with. But it is right that we do so. A book is not the result of just one person, but also all those who assist, encourage, stimulate and provoke. I would like to thank all those involved at Christian Focus Publications, especially my editor Colin Duriez. I love the congregation in St Peter's, who provide constant stimulus and proof of the gospel. They have put up with me for twenty-one years and yet still we love one another, warts and all! I thank my non-Christian friends, especially Gary McLelland, for their robust and stimulating critiques. David Meredith, minister of Smithton Free Church in Inverness, has always encouraged me, even in the most difficult of times. Dr John Ellis has the sharpest mind I know but, more than that, is a living example of how to wrestle with the most difficult questions in a Christ-like and gracious manner. Without his interaction this book would have been a lot poorer.

The writing of this book would not have happened were it not for the dedicated and skilful medical staff at Ninewells Hospital in Dundee, whose care and skill saved my life – or, as my surgeon Mr Shimi put it, 'God saved your life; we were just his instruments.' I am very thankful for all God's instruments, none more so than my family. My wife Annabel is my lover, best friend, partner and a tower of strength for me; our son Andrew, daughter Becky (and husband Pete), and our teenage bundle of joy, Emma-Jane, are truly the Lord's blessing.

There are countless others whose lives, sorrows, joys, deeds and words have shaped my life and therefore my perceptions and words. I thank them all whilst accepting, of course, that any mistakes in this book are entirely my responsibility. I believe that these various people are part of the rich tapestry of life woven together by the One who was, and is, and is to come. In Christ, alone, our hope is found.

David Robertson
Dundee
2013

If you have any questions or comments about this book please feel free to contact David at david@solas-cpc.org

Christian Focus Publications

Our mission statement –

STAYING FAITHFUL
In dependence upon God we seek to impact the world through literature faithful to His infallible Word, the Bible. Our aim is to ensure that the Lord Jesus Christ is presented as the only hope to obtain forgiveness of sin, live a useful life and look forward to heaven with Him.

Our Books are published in four imprints:

CHRISTIAN
FOCUS

popular works including biographies, commentaries, basic doctrine and Christian living.

CHRISTIAN
HERITAGE

books representing some of the best material from the rich heritage of the church.

MENTOR

books written at a level suitable for Bible College and seminary students, pastors, and other serious readers. The imprint includes commentaries, doctrinal studies, examination of current issues and church history.

CF4•K

children's books for quality Bible teaching and for all age groups: Sunday school curriculum, puzzle and activity books; personal and family devotional titles, biographies and inspirational stories – Because you are never too young to know Jesus!

Christian Focus Publications Ltd,
Geanies House, Fearn, Ross-shire,
IV20 1TW, Scotland, United Kingdom.
www.christianfocus.com